Conversations
with
Stones

An Earth Lodge Collection of Crystals
for Healing, Meditation and
Manifestation

By Maya Cointreau

An Earth Lodge® Publication
Roxbury, Connecticut

*** This book is not intended to take the place of proper health care and expertise. Please seek qualified professional care for health problems. ***

Printed & Published in the U.S.A.
by Earth Lodge®
ISBN 978-1-944396-13-8

Earth Lodge® is a registered trademark.

For the Crystalline Club,
my fellow rockhounds,

Thank you for joining me on this
ever-expanding journey through
the spiral of stones.

Crystalline Connections

Crystals, or Stone People, have been here since the beginning, watching our planet form among the stars, seeing our earthly plants breath their first breath, applauding us as we took our first steps. Each crystal has its own unique spirit, and its own driving mission. The stones have worked so hard to be where they are. They have walked with the fairies, waited under desert sun, slept in cavernous darkness and tumbled down streams to reach you.

Since I was a young girl, I adored the stone people. I would pick out the most interesting ones from our gravel driveway, and hunt for gems in the woods. I would display them among the flowers at home, making wee fairy gardens, or knock on neighbors doors to try to sell them the prettiest ones while other children sold lemonade from their driveways.

Six years ago, I began to lead a group of women each month in meditation with high vibration stones. We called ourselves the Crystalline Club, and spent our days between meetings communing with our stones.

This book is the offspring of that group union and contains information for sixty eight stones. Accompanying each one you will find a message channeled directly from the crystals, followed by its

1

metaphysical uses and a meditation to help you connect to the energy of that stone.

Many of the stones in this book are quite rare or unusual. Every stone is unique, with its own energy signature and message for the bearer. Small or large, each stone is a powerful tool for connecting with the divine and shifting your vibration.

You might wonder if you can truly connect with a stones even if you do not have it in your possession. You can. By simply holding the intent to link with its energy, you will form a connection. If you wish, a simple internet search for an image of the stone can help strengthen your visualization and intent.

Working with Crystals

Minerals have been used by healers for thousands of years. Crystals and rocks carry the soothing, grounding energy of the Earth within them. Each stone has a different crystalline structure which resonates at a difference frequency, and each frequency targets a different healing energy. Some crystals are used for healing, some for calming, some for joy and some for protection. Many great books exist about crystals: two of my favorites are "The Crystal Bible" by Judy Hall and "Love is in the Earth" by Melody. The first is a beautifully illustrated reference with all the most common stones, well-suited for beginners, and the second is a vast compendium of practically every stone ever named.

Supporting stones can be placed near your sleeping area, in or near your drinking water (use care, as some crystals can be toxic or dissolve in water, such as malachite, sulphur and selenite), worn around your neck or carried in your pocket. They can be placed under the table when you are conducting hands-on healing work, or placed near your tinctures and remedies for empowerment. Used in the environment, crystals heal harmonic discord and can even ameliorate EMF waves. They are soothing and beneficial to all beings, on many levels.

Collecting crystals can be an addictive pastime, their energies are so uplifting and expansive, generally altering our vibration in positive ways. When you are looking for new stones, whether it be on a walk in the woods or in a metaphysical store or at a jewelry expo, let your senses guide you. Listen to your inner mind and pay attention to any small tugs you may feel. Not only can we feel crystals, but they can feel us. The right stones will call to you.

Many people like to clear or purify their stone of previous owners' energies. This can be done by placing the stone in a bowl or cool "sea" water (salt is very purifying) or letting the light of the sun or moon shine on it for a prescribed amount of time, be it hours or days. Sunlight can fade the colors of some crystals, such as amethyst and fluorite, so use care.

Before working with a new stone, quiet your mind. Sit with the stone in your hand and allow yourself to feel its energies. You can program a crystal by conversing with it and asking it to help you achieve a certain goal, chanting your intentions over it, or stroking the stone while you state your purpose. Place the stone on a piece of paper on which you've written a prayer or goal, or put it in your pocket or on your alter or under your pillow, and allow it time to work its own special creation magic.

To make a crystal elixir or essence simply place the stone on or near a bowl of water and allow the water time to "infuse" with the stone's energies. To strengthen the elixir, make it during a full or new moon, a solar event or thunderstorm, or surround it with an empowering crystal grid of multiple quartz points. When you are ready, remove the crystal, and store the water in a dark glass container, mixed with vinegar (white or apple cider) in a 50/50 solution. Vodka or Brandy may also be used. If in doubt, ask your local devas, overlighting angels, or fairies for their advice. This solution is called the "mother essence". Any extra, unused essence water can be used to water you plants to great advantage.

When you wish to make dosage bottles to use the crystal essence, fill the bottles with ¼ vinegar and ¾ pure water, and add 12 drops of mother essence per ounce. If you are making a combination bottle which will hold multiple essences, add 3 drops per ounce of each mother essence. Working on an energetic level, crystal elixirs remain dormant until they are needed, so that whichever ones are relevant at the time a combination formula is taken will be activated and work for the user.

Crystal elixirs work on similar principals to homeopathy, and as such cannot interfere with medication or exacerbate conditions. They can only improve a situation, never harm. Crystal essences can be taken by the dropper-full under the tongue or in a glass or water. They may be placed next to the bed while you sleep or in your pocket during the day. Their beneficial harmonies are far-reaching, and do not need to be ingested to exert their happy influences. Try placing a few drops in the water bottle you carry throughout the day, or in your drink with dinner. Most importantly, use them with love and affection, for they will bloom under good attentions.

A Meditation for Accessing Any Crystalline Spirit

To begin, sit comfortably and hold your stone in your hands, taking three deep breaths.

Breathe in, and breathe out.

Relax your muscles.

Breathe in and out.

In and out.

Calm your mind, release your thoughts.

Allow your entire being to relax.

Easy. Easy.

Calm.

Feel your consciousness sinking, safe and slow, as you go deeper and deeper into the darkness of your inner mind, as you reach your inner point of stillness.

Here in the center of your being, deep in your mind's eye, see yourself quiet, at peace, and whole.

See yourself stand up, and walk through the darkness into a cool cave deep in the earth.

You feel safe here, secure, and very protected.

You run your hand along the walls of the cavern and can feel the vast wisdom of the ages surrounding you.

In the middle of the cave, you see the great mother of the stone you are holding, the piece from which your own was birthed, and you approach it with reverence.

It welcomes you to the cavern, and asks you to sit and speak with it.

You show the mother stone the small piece you hold in your hand, and ask her to bless it.

You ask the stones if there is a particular name your piece would like to be addressed by, and introduce yourself. You explain what your intentions are, and what you are currently desiring in your life or needing help.

Ask the stones what way would be best for you to work with your piece, and if it has any particular messages for you.

Thank the mother and your stone for their blessings and their help.

Stand up, and walk back the way you came. See yourself deep in the darkness, deep in your body, once again.

Breathe deeply.

In.

And out.

In and out.

Relax.

Return.

Gridwork with Crystals

A crystal grid is a number of crystals arranged into a particular geometric form creating a particular energy field. The simplest crystal grid is a triangle formed of three crystals. When you form a crystal grid, the crystals should be of equal strength and similar size. You can form a grid of any geometric shape or symbol. Each shape and symbol carries its own symbolism and uses. You may use a grid to charge or empower any object, including another crystal or yourself, by placing the object in the center of the grid. Try focusing your intent by choosing tarot or oracle cards, or writing a list of desires, and placing them within the center of the grid.

"The Crystal Grids we will focus on are arrangements of charged crystals dedicated to a particular purpose such as sending healing energy or focusing a manifestation or For Earth healing or to bring in or broadcast specific frequencies of energy into a certain area. They are a way of creating a continuous flow of energy for a specific purpose on a larger scale than by just programming a single crystal. They are often used to send remote healing to others , as part of rituals for Earth healing or peace, for manifestation procedures and broadcasting affirmations and personal goals.

They are often used to magnify, focus and or prolong a treatment using energy work such as Reiki . The quartz and crystal healing shakti from the crystal empowerments can also be focused using a crystal grid or used to charge one. Some grids are made so that you can place food or clothes inside or on or near them to clear and charge them. You can put a grid under your bed or massage table. You might put a small prosperity grid in your cash drawer at work or put a grid in your flower garden.

Some grids are simple circles others are based on traditions of sacred geometry and/or forms like the tree of Life , Mercaba , Ankh, infinity sign or even the peace symbol. Some grids are simply a number of stones placed in parallel rows.

There is even a form where a real grid is made of copper wire and crystals are placed on this , some of these are made large enough for a person to lay comfortably inside. These are sometimes made as a floor for a large copper pyramid.

You may also place the crystals on a paper marked with a diagram of the layout for the grid or with a traditional sacred form such as the star of Solomon, The Sephiroth or tree of life , the infinity symbol or on or around an image of a symbol such as the antakarana or a Goddess or an emblem of your spiritual path.

Grids may be left permanently or until their purpose is fulfilled and are usually recharged and dedicated fairly often. A specific schedule for this recharging is impossible to set as it will vary from grid to grid.

You will want to place your grid in a location where it is not easily disturbed yet is accessible for recharging Your grid may hold its charge longer without recharging if it is placed in a location where it gets some sun or moonlight."

By aligning the crystals into a geometric form, they form pillars or vortices of light and energy within the center: it is with this energy field that you are working. Eventually you may want to build crystal grids under your bed or chair, or on a specific part of your body that may be ailing you: wait until you feel ready to process the energy generated by crystals to try this. If you feel you have taken in too much energy afterward, try holding a grounding crystal such as agate, carnelian or obsidian; take a salt bath; or take a walk in nature.

Crystal grids can absorb imbalanced energies and are excellent tools for healing but as always you should clear the crystals using sun or moonlight, running water, salt water, smudge or earth. Always ask their permission before you conduct this sort of work. And enjoy yourself!

Triangle: Thought and emotion projection, The Divine Trinities.

Square: Balance, Strength, Foundation, 4 directions/elements.

Circle: Perfection, Protection, Source Energy, Completion

Pentagram: 5 elements, Spirit, increase (upright), decrease (inverted).

Hexagram: Balance Male and Female energies, Polarity work, Astral Travel.

Pyramid: Energy raising, Thought Focusing, Projection, Protection

8- or 12-Spoked Wheel: These grids are used to invoke the seasons and the zodiac. They empower the grid with all the powers or energies of a solar cycle. Buddhist monks use these wheels.

13-spoked Wheel: This grid invokes the lunar cycle.

Spiral: Reiki Energy, Increasing Energy, Goddess Energy

The Crystalline Merkaba

"The merkaba is perhaps one of the most accurate representations humanity has of divine energy. It spins, it flows, it grows in all directions at all times. It balances and harmonizes, and takes you where you want to be, into the life you are wanting. It does this both in the physical and the spiritual dimensions: yes, you can actually travel with the merkaba. Or you can use it to become who you want to be. The merkaba is the infinite circulating flow of the divine trinity and the four directions, the four elements. It is all, all at once."

A merkaba is a star tetrahedron, a three dimensional 8 pointed star made from two triangular pyramids, one pointing up and the other down. It harmonizes male and female energy, much like a Yin/Yang symbol. The star of David is a two dimensional version of a merkaba, and was reputed to have been painted on the shields of the armies of King David as a symbol of divine protection.

The merkaba does, in fact, step down source energy into the physical and is a representational invocation of "as above, so below". The pyramid pointing upwards connects us to heavenly universal energy and represents yang, positive energy flows. The pyramid pointing downward connects to the earth and resonates with yin, negative energy flows.

The merkaba is emblematic of the greater energy field that surrounds our body beyond our field auric field. Most people who can view auras see them as a diffuse egg-shaped color field around our body that changes colors and ranges in size from 6-36 inches. Beyond our Aura we have the etheric field, and further out we have an immense energy field, reputed to grow up to 55 feet across and saucer-shaped when it is fully energized: our merkaba, our light body. A properly functioning merkaba field is not static, but comprised of the two tetrahedrons spinning incredibly fast in opposite directions, creating a light body that is capable of great feats, including interdimensional and interstellar travel.

Merkaba are believed to be the same divine light vehicle used by ascended masters to connect with and reach those in tune with the higher realms. It is thought by many that the "chariots of fire" mentioned in the bible are these same vehicles. Mer-Ka-Ba literally means light-spirit-body in Hebrew, denoting the harmonious activation of the three fields. When your merkaba is active you are tapped in to all Source energy and locked into the Earth's living matrix. Your DNA is fully turned on and the potential for immortality and time travel are there. Your soul excels. Your body heals itself and you have the potential for limitless creation.

Meditating with Your Merkaba

Your merkaba is in constant communication and connection with all of Source. It is your creative matrix that allows you to combine your soul intention with the spark of god-energy and literally create your reality however you want. Like a crystal, it can be programmed through meditation and by setting your intention. All that is required is for your merkaba to be actively spinning, which is done through breathing exercises and habit, and by simply instructing your merkaba as to what you want it to do. You are the only one on earth who can work with or program your merkaba. No other human or healer may influence the programming of your merkaba, although a healer may work on your breathwork and energy patterning to help facilitate merkaba activation.

Most people choose to pattern their merkabas in one of two ways: active or reactive. Active programming is very yang in energy, task specific, detailed and proactive: if there is negative energy in a room emanating from a person or geopathic stress, you can program your merkaba to deflect it. If you are wanting a specific job, your merkaba can reach into the energy matrix of the Earth and help conspire to create this specific reality. Reactive, female patterning is more reactive and open than the active patterning, it tends to use overarching instructions such as "I program my merkaba to flow with ease in this physical earth reality and to see that all my needs and desires are fulfilled for the highest good of all involved." There is less judgment of specific situations and more acceptance and anticipation of the synchronicity. Neutral programming is the way of the Tao, neither reactive nor proactive, it simply is. Situations come and go with equal lack of prejudice or preference. This sort of programming is common in those pursuing a monastic life.

Let us begin:

First let us see the tetrahedrons surrounding your body: the male pyramid points upwards and begins at your knees, extending several feet above your head. The female pyramid extends downwards from your shoulders and reaches several feet below your own feet. Are your pyramids spinning? Let us activate them now so that each pyramid spins in a different direction – the male pyramid spins from left to right around your body, and the female pyramid spins from right to left around your body. Together, they energize your meridians more fully. As they spin, see them create a light field around your body, growing larger and larger in a saucer like shape expanded by the centrifugal force of the merkaba.

Breathe in, and out, in and out, a circular pattern that further fuels your merkaba.

Now think about abou how you, personally, would like to pattern your merkaba. How will you put your personal computer to work for you? Take some time to focus your attention on the matter, and set your intention with your merkaba now.

Know that whatever you have intended, your merkaba is now working on it completely, without deviation of failure.

As you have willed it, so shall it be.

Now slowly take your focus off your merkaba, and return to your aura, see the healthy glow all around you, your chakras in tune, your cells turned on to their full potential. You are energized and you are well.

Return now, into your body, and be ready for LIFE!

Alexandrite

"Alexandrite is a stone of JOY. This is the stone to bring you into alignment with your true self. This is the stone that helps you be at one with your higher self, to be at one with all of you, and all of us. For this reason, alexandrite has received a reputation as a channeler's stone. It is because it holds pure source energy. Pure Source YOU."

This rare gemstone is named after the Russian tsar Alexander II (1818-1881), the very first crystals having been discovered in April 1834 in the emerald mines near the Tokovaya River in the Urals. The discovery was made on the day the future tsar came of age. Since it shows both red and green, the principal colors of old Imperial Russia, it inevitably became the national stone of tsarist Russia.

Alexandrite is very rare indeed and hardly ever used in modern jewelry. The most sensational feature about this stone is its surprising ability to change its color. Green or bluish-green in daylight, alexandrite turns a soft shade of red, purplish-red or raspberry red in incandescent light.

Alexandrite is very scarce: this is due to its chemical composition. It is basically a chrysoberyl, but differs from other chrysoberyls in that it not only contains iron and titanium, but also chromium as a major impurity. And it is this very element which accounts for the spectacular color change. Like many other gemstones, alexandrite emerged millions of years ago in a metamorphic environment. But unlike many others, its formation required specific geological conditions. The chemical elements

18

beryllium (a major constituent in chrysoberyl) and chromium (the coloring agent in alexandrite) have contrasting chemical characteristics and do not as a rule occur together, usually being found in contrasting rock types. Not only has Nature brought these contrasting rock types into contact with each other, but a lack of the chemical element silica (the second most common element in the Earth's crust) is also required to prevent the growth of emerald. This geological scenario has occurred only rarely in the Earth's history and, as a result, alexandrite crystals are very scarce indeed.

Alexandrite is considered a stone of very good omen. In critical situations it is supposed to strengthen the wearer's intuition, and thus help him or her find new ways forward in situations where logic will not provide an answer. Alexandrite is also reputed to aid creativity and inspire the imagination.

Alexandrites are stones of joy, and have a close connection to the higher realms of source energy. Alexandrite shows us that the rapturous energies of source are here at every moment, and the level of our connection to Source shifts our reality: the quality of our reality shifts depending upon our willingness to receive the light and joy of Source. Alexandrite allows us to move past sadness or self-pity and find our point of power in the current moment. It is excellent for those who procrastinate or who are held back by fear. It opens the heart and third eye chakras, and offers hope and light in the darkest of times. It can be used to attract wealth and manifest dreams and desires. It connects one directly to the sensations and being-ness of Divine Love and Joy.

It hold Akashic and Atlantean knowledge, and assists one to recover the knowledge from past lives, particularly if one is searching for priestly or divine records. On a physical level it stimulates the pineal and pituitary glands, and benefits brain function.

A Meditation from Alexandrite

Go Outside.

Sit on the grass in the center of some trees.

Close your eyes. Relax. If you are with others, sit in a circle and link hands.

Close your eyes, breathe deeply. Feel your consciousness rising as each breathe brings you more and more into the moment.

Listen to the birds. Hear the wind rustling in the trees. Feel the earth pulsing, your heart aligning with the rhythms of the earth mother and the earth energies running through the circle.

Let your self come into alignment with your true self. Listen to your self, feel your happiness. What messages does your self have for you? How best may alexandrite serve you?

Give gratitude to your self. Be easy and happy in the knowledge that you are closer to your self than you ever have been and that you are never alone, that you are one with all and all is one with you.

Hold the joy, and release the moment. Return.

Angelite

"Angelite is here to ease the fear. Angelite blesses and bestows grace. It calms the spirit, because it is spirit. Angelite brings in the knowledge of Source records and helps place you directly in the flow of Source. It raises the vibration of your energy flow."

Angelite, or Anhydrite, is a fairly common stone found in Peru, and is believed by most to be a compressed or non-crystalline form of celestite. It is a high vibration stone that connects with angels and the higher realms. It helps induce a state of calm and peace, so that one can integrate ascension patterns with the energetic flow and traffic of daily life.

It works directly with the upper chakras, beginning with the throat chakra, to enhance communication with our higher selves. This, in turn, eases communication with those around us. Angelite is often used to boost meditative states and encourage guidance from the higher realms. Channeling and psychic abilities both receive long-term benefits from the use of angelite.

Angelite enhances compassion and understanding, and helps counteract bullying and meanness. Prone to angry outbursts or insensitive comments? Give angelite a try.

Physically, angelite may decrease pain, heal trauma, benefit the thyroid and pituitary glands, and relieve headaches, throat and ear issues.

Note: Do not immerse in water or wear when bathing: angelite is a soft stone that transforms to gypsum when exposed to water.

A Meditation with Angelite

To begin, sit comfortably and hold your stone in your hands, taking a deep breath in.

And then breathe out.

Let's relax and let of the day. Let go of things you said. Let go of what you need to do.

Let go. Just let go.

Breathe in. And breathe out.

And let go.

Feel yourself rising up into the blue, blue sky of summer. You are surrounded by sky. Bathed in light. You feel clean. You feel clear. You are at peace, and filled with radiant energy.

Your stone vibrates in your hand, releasing bursts of energy that fill your soul with light. The sky, the stone, you, you are all as one. You are all at peace, and fully energized. You are all radiant, and filled with source. You are One.

Messages come to you directly from source, with no lapse in time or meaning, because you are as one with the flow of source.

Now, your stone becomes a stone once again, and is still and quiet. The light around you eases. You slowly sink back down, down through the clouds, down from the sky, down through the air, down to the earth, down to this room, down into your body, down into your seat, into your body, down to your toes.

You return, and you are calm, you are healthy, and you are well.

Return.

Apatite

"People mistake the stillness of water for calm, but we are not calm. We are deep. We hold the mysteries. We hold the energies of the unfathomable and the potentials of the void."

Blue is the color of life force. It is the color of that which animates and holds together all life energy on your planet, all that is alive in the universe, all that thinks, feels, moves, grows and glows. We are not calm. We are not tranquil. We are that which animates, that which glows. Hold us, and feel yourself

re-align with the energy of Source. Use us to heal your gridwork, to rework your DNA, to channel your energies in more positive ways."

Apatite is said to enhance one's insight, learning abilities and imagination, and to give increased self-confidence. It also is said to help achieve deeper states of meditation, and helps to restore clear thoughts. It creates a willingness to let go of useless aspects of life, people and objects. Continued use of apatite is told to produce a spiritual state of unconditional love, thus it is related to service and to humanitarian pursuits.

Blue apatite connects to a very high level of spiritual guidance, that is not often reached. Being associated with the throat chakra, it facilitates public speaking, enhances group communication, and opens the throat chakra. It will heal the heart, and emotional dis-ease.

Blue Apatite can help to effectively work within the dream state to form solutions to perplexing problems. Those who are overemotional can benefit from Apatite's ability to highlight logical solutions and induce calm states of mind.

Blue Apatite can help to develop psychic gifts and connect the user to higher levels of spiritual guidance. Use Blue Apatite to deepen and maintain focus in meditation. Blue Apatite can also initiate, stimulate, and/or increase the development of psychic abilities, such as clairvoyance and clairaudience. Apatite is attuned to the future, yet helps us connect to past lives.

Physically, it acts as a hunger suppressant. Simply wear or carry a piece with you throughout the day. Blue Apatite also eliminates blockages and returns the body to balance. Blue Apatite can cleanse the aura of cluttered energies, bringing a renewed sensation to the body. Blue Apatite is a good stone to help balance the chakras, as well as the energies of Yin and Yang. It heals the glands, meridians and organs, and overcomes hypertension. It balances the physical, emotional, mental and spiritual bodies as well as the chakras. Used with other crystals, apatite will facilitate the results. Apatite is reputed in mystical lore to physically apatite assist with nail problems, allergies, arthritis, bones, muscles, nervous system.

Fun Fact: Apatite is the mineral that makes up the teeth in all vertebrate animals as well as their bones.

A Meditation with Apatite

Breathe in the air. Breathe out the fire. Let go all the fire and smoke from the day, breathe it out, let it out, let it go. Breathe in the air. Fill up your lungs, your bodies, your cells. Fill your bodies and mind with clear, pure air and ether, with spirit and glow.

You are sitting on an important energy spot, a place of ancient power. There is an earth-well here, a ley line, a large piece of the power grid that creates the form of the earth herself. See the line running under your feet, through this room, running parallel with the road outside. You are connected to many things, many places, when you sit here. You are connect to all the power places on the Earth. The gridwork of the earth runs everywhere in fine, electric blue lines, and some of these lines are stronger, wider, more turned on and tapped into by you humans. These are the places where humans have learned how to connect to the powers of Source, where humans used to be able to travel between lands without the use of fossil fuels or vehicles, where time and space can cease to exist and you may become one with ALL THAT IS, in the blink of an eye.

So you sit here, on this blue line. What shall you do? Who shall you become? Begin your journey by seeing your own body covered with a fine blue gridwork, and heal any empty spaces or broken lines that you see. Hold your stone in your hand and use the power of the stone, which is naturally aligned with all gridwork, to align your energies with the ley line below you. As you heal your gridwork, feel your connection to the earth and Source grow ever stronger, ever more pure.

You are one with all. The energy of source flows through you and around you in one strong wave of energy. There is no separation. Feel yourself within the wave, and open your mind to your stone. Now is the time to receive any messages or information your new piece may have for you. Open your mind to source and be ready to receive.

You are one with all. You are whole. Now feel your body. Wiggle your toes. Open and close your hands. Feel your breath. That's right – breathe in, and breathe out. Breathe as slow or as fast as you like. Feel your body. Revel in the tool that you have received from source, this great physical vehicle that carries all the power and potentials of the grid.

Breathe in the air. Breathe in your power. You are Whole. Thank your stone, and close your meditation as you open your eyes.

Apophyllite

"The Angelic realms have been working with you, preparing you, for your future, for your now, for who you are becoming. Most of this work has been going on behind the scenes, without you realizing it – while you are sleeping, relaxing, working. All beneath the realm of consciousness. Now is the time to work more consciously. When you work with us, you will hear the angels directly. When you work with us the truest aspects of your soul will be unveiled. We lift the curtain, revealing all that was hidden. We illuminate the darkness, flooding it with the light that was always there."

Apophyllite is a class of abundant phyllosilicates that contains high amounts of silicate and oxygen. It is most often clear or white, but can also appear green, blue, purple, pink, yellow or brown, and often forms natural pyramid shapes.

Apophyllite is most well-known for its use in amplifying activity in the third eye and crown chakras. It is prized by many for its ability to enhance astral travel, telepathy, remte viewing, meditation and channeling. Along with Angelite, it is a favorite stone for connecting with the Angelic Realm.

Apophyllite tends to enchance organization and planning skills, while showing the truth of what is needed so that the future may be prepared for more effectively.

Physically, crystal healers use Apophyllite to remedy eye and respiratory ailments, such as eyestrain and asthma.

Meditation with Apophyllite

Close your eyes and relax, holding one apophyllite in each hand.

(If you only have one stone, place it on your crown chakra, if seated, or third eye, if lying down.)

Breathe in, and breathe out. Relax. Let your worries go. All is well. Breathe in, and breathe out. Relax. Unwind. Feel yourself unwinding, opening.

Open yourself to the void of creation, where all is possible. Open yourself to the future. See yourself in the well of creation, where the world can be as you make it. How will you create your domain? What will you include in your world? What will you remove? Imagine your domain, your reality, your home, your life. See the truth of where your desires would take you. Is it good? Is it kind? Is it needed? Now spend a little more time, further tweaking and arranging your domain.

Good.

Now, I want you to spend a little more time with your stones. What are their names? What are their desires? How can they work with you best? How do they fit into the domain you have created?

Good.

Now relax. Breathe in, and breathe out. Gather up your domain, breath it into your body. That's right, breathe it into you, take it all in. Breathe it in. Now come back into this realm, back into your body. And breathe out. Breathe out your new domain, knowing that as you do so you are sowing the seeds for your new reality. Breathe out, and know that it is good.

Good.

Now, return.

Apple Green Opal

"We are quiet. We are still. Unlike our flashy brothers and sisters, we cool the fires in your hearts, and encourage a slow and steady burn. We facilitate the transformation from impatient youth to wise crone, without the loss of energy, stamina and wit that your society associates with aging. We bring energized wisdom, the brilliance of a mature sun. Old wounds and personal issues fade away as you become true Christ-consciousness, as you become open heart, open mind."

Opal is a non-crystalline mineral formed of a combination of silica and water formed into a hardened gel. Most opals contain between 5 and 15% water by weight, although some contain even more. For this reason, opals should not be subjected to abrupt changes in temperature, which may cause them to crack, or extreme heat, which may cause them to dry out and crack.

In India, the opal was associated with the Rainbow Goddess, while in Arab nations it was believed to be an amulet of invisibility.

The silica structure of opal makes it an optimal stone of transformation for the new age as we evolve into crystalline beings. The water contained within allows us to transform old karma, emotional wounds and anger into wisdom, love and compassion. It helps us accept change gracefully and with ease, like a rock in a stream. They are also very good aids in meditation, astral travel, and work with the Akashic Records (ie: past life retrievals).

Green opal is considered especially beneficial to the overall health of the physical body and may help fight off viral and bacterial infections. It energizes both the body and mind and helps the bearer regain a fresh sense of perspective in difficult situations. It is believed by many that opal can help fight off depression and will strengthen one's will to live.

All opals are traditionally believed to be stones of luck and good fortune. There is a newer, modern superstitions about opals as stones of misfortune, but these rumors originated from the gem industry's effort to sell more diamonds. Opals are wonderful wishing stones. They will project and magnify the emotions of the wearer and help to transform emotions and desires into concrete reality (make sure you are in a good state of mind when you work with opal!)

A Meditation with Apple Green Opal

Hold the opal in your hand. Close your eyes and feel the opal's aura, its energy. Breathe in and feel your aura expanding. Breathe out, and feel the opal's aura expand with you. You breathe in and out, and both your auras continue to expand. They begin to merge and comingle, to become one. The stone itself begins to soften and become one with your body, to heal your crystalline form and soothe your cellular structure. DNA healing begins to take place on every level of your being. Opal is here to work with you. To heal you. To improve you.

Take some time now to sit with opal and feel the flow of source gather and pool within you, feeding your every awakening soul and body.

***

Now breathe in, and breathe out. Allow your aura to slowly return to its optimal state. The stone separates from your aura, slowly and easily. You hold it in your hand. You hold the key to your future in your hands. What doors will you unlock?

Return, and begin you life again, fresh and renewed.

Aqua Onyx

"Aqua Onyx heals the pathways of the soul as it enters the body. It facilitates a greater companionship between the two modalities, soul energy and physical being. Old wounds of the heart are healed, and karma is released gracefully. The body becomes stronger, a worthy temple for the soul to house itself in. This is the secret of why so many have made their drinkware out of it – water drunk from an onyx cup is especially healthful and empowering. Likewise, water infused with onyx will have a strong, good effect on the body."

Onyx is a type of chalcedony with straight banding. It comes in a myriad of colors from brown, to black to green and white. Onyx is believed by many to hold the memories of those who have worn or touched it. In fact, onyx simply connects you to your higher self with greater efficiency, so that you can access these sorts of records through Source and mass consciousness. Because it connects you so readily with your higher self, onyx is a great companion stone to aid in decision making or following your life path. Are you ready to become the master of your own future?

Onyx is a slow-moving stone, energetically speaking. The longer it is worn or used, the stronger its power will build, with cumulative restorative effects. Onyx is particularly well-suited to healing skin, bone and cellular tissues, or anyone needing more strength and balance in their mind or body. It is very grounding, protective and may enhance sexual energy. As a master harmonizer, onyx balances the masculine and the feminine.

Onyx benefits from weekly or monthly cleansing using either salted water or earth burial.

Meditation with Aqua Onyx

This meditation is about possibilities. Close your eyes and relax.

As you breathe in, and out, in and out, feel your tension slip away. Feel the energy of the sun filling you with a pure, healthy glow. As you exhale, release old thought patterns and belief systems. Identify some of things you do not wish to carry with you into this new year, into your new present and future. Exhale them out. Breathe them out. Release your old fears. Release your old patterns. Let go of grievances and dramas.

Now, hold your stone to your solar plexus, and feel the energy of the earth fill you with power. You are the creator of your entire universe. What is it that you would like to be doing? Where is it that you would like to be going? How do you envision your present self learning and growing. Take time now to visualize all that you are intending for yourself. Take time to see and to feel yourself becoming happier and more relaxed, fulfilled and joy-full.

Now speak with your stone. How may it assist you during the coming weeks?

Breathe in your new reality. Breathe it fully, breathe it deeply. Feel your power and radiance expanding and be-coming.

You are well. You are fulfilled.

Return.

Axinite

"Bring out your dead! Release your inhibitions, air out your old ambitions and desires! We light up the darkest recesses of your soul and your memory, we show you what you have hidden away from your conscious mind, and allow you to reclaim the truth. Bring out the dreams you thought had passed away. Get creative. Get happy! We will breathe new life into the gray."

Axinite is a calcium aluminium borosilicate found in metamorphic rocks. It is pyroelectric and piezoelectric, meaning it will generate electricity under pressure or heat. Difficult to find in store, axinite is found in Russia, Mexico, the USA and France.

Axinite is a grounding, uplifting stone that helps us shift negative energy into positive. It is extremely useful when you are trying to instigate change in your life or simply looking to shift to a new level. Use it to enhance creative thinking and manifest your ambitions. Because it helps us go with the flow more easily and adapt, axinite can be helpful when we change time zones or are trying to create new routines in our life.

Axinite helps us recover old memories, and to assimilate thought and memories from various stages of evolution or vibration. This can be very useful for helping with dream recall or recovering deep meditation and trance experiences. Better yet, axinite helps us tap into the Akash and access ALL memories, all knowledge. It reveals the truth, making it useful in legal situations or whenever someone might not be telling the whole story.

Physically, it can boost circulation through the lower extremities as is brings up earth energies through all the chakras and helps activate the third eye. Energizing the entire body, it benefits the immune system while increasing strength and endurance.

A Meditation with Axinite

Breathe in. Breathe out. Relax.

You are surrounded by a warm glow, a light glow. Feel the warmth traveling up from your feet, up your legs, through your body, up to your head.

Breathe in, and out.

You feel warm, and you feel comfortable. You feel secure and relaxed.

Go deep into your mind, and relax. What is the question foremost in your mind today? What do you want to know?

The answer is within your grasp. Simply hold your stone to your temple, and relax. Let the answer come to you. You already know it. You have always known it. All the answers are already within you. You simply need to ask, and relax.

Spend some time now with your stone, and find out how you may best work together. What does axinite want you to know? How would it like you to use it? Does it have a name or a special message for you? Spend some time now with your stone, and relax.

All is well. Thank your stone, and know that all will be well. You hold all the answers within you. You are the key. You are the key.

All is well.

Return.

Bastnäsite

"Can you feel the rhythm? We are going to connect you to the beat of the earth, bring you fully down into your body so you can really live passionately and radiantly. Dance. Play. Make Love. Be in your body and energize everything you touch. Wear us skin to skin for best effect."

Bastnäsite, or Bastnaesite, was discovered and named for the Bastnä mines of Sweden in 1838, although the best specimens often come from Pakistan in the Zagi mountains. It can also be found in small concentrations in Greece, Turkey, Mongolia, California, Ontario, Russia and several other countries. It is a carbonate-fluoride mineral that contains cerium, a rare earth mineral. The higher quality specimens from Pakistan often change color in different lighting, most often from red to orange or yellow, from green to yellow, or from yellow to orange.

Bastnäsite tends to exercise its powerful healing energies upon the root and heart chakras, creating a strong harmonic resonance in the body with one's life path upon earth. Bastnäsite removes fear from the body and takes us out of survival mode so that we can fully enjoy life on earth as physical beings.

It relaxes the mind and enlivens the body, while strengthening, activating and aligning all layers of the body: physical, etheric, auric, astral.

Many people use it to connect with the fae and elemental energies of the planet. Use it to reaffirm your connection to Mother Earth.

Physically, use it to return vitality to the body, increase strength and improve disease related to the heart, circulation, and sexuality. May also benefit addiction.

Meditation with Bastnäsite

Hold your stone to your heart and breathe in slowly, aligning with its energy. In and out. Breathing slowly and deeply. In and out.

Feel the radiance and the joy of Bastnäsite flowing through your body, radiating out from your heart. The energy pools in your root chakra, pulsing and growing.

You feel strong. You feel alive. You are fearless. The world is yours.

You knew the world was yours when you were born. You have forgotten. Remember who you are. You are strong. You are powerful. You are alive. The world is yours.

Now spend some time with your stone. Ask if it has a name or any special ways it would like to be used by you this month. Ask how you can best assimilate its healing energies into your life.

All is well.

Breathe out.

Breathe in.

Return.

Birds Eye Rhyolite

"See what we see. See to the core of things. See through the veil, through the drama, through the illusions of your reality and go deeply into your cellular makeup, into the energetic patterning of the world."

Birdseye Rhyolite is mined primarily in Mexico, forming in a massive rhyolitic deposit with spherical formations in red, cream, gray and pink colors. Rhyolite is a fine grained volcanic rock, chemically similar to granite and composed essentially of feldspar and quartz. Rhyolite can look very different, depending on how it erupts. Because of its varied formational traits it represents change, variety and progress. It sparks creativity in individuals who are ready to move forward and make things happen in their life. It allows us to reach out and beyond our capabilities of what we think we can achieve by helping us to break through the mental barriers and to reach a profound and joyous state of knowing to follow the right path.

Rhyolite shows us how to relish in the vast potential within ourselves. This is a stone used for meditation, focusing on the present moment and resolving issues not yet complete. It also integrates the past with the present for past life healing, increases self-esteem and leads to a full acceptance of self. It can help one allow other people into their lives, even if one has been reclusive or solitary. It is also a stone of protection.

As a healing stone, rhyolite fortifies the body's natural resistance, gives strength and improves muscle tone. Rhyolite is a stone of regeneration and help you to look and feel younger. It is good for all skin problems, especially those with viral origins. It will aid fight infection and is good for animal bites and insect stings. It will help speed up emotional healing after a nervous breakdown or trauma.

Because this stone vibrates under the number 4 which is about hard work, good foundations and structure, many believe that Rhyolite will assist one in working towards their goals in a proficient manner. This stone will not allow you to simply give up on your goals or life dreams, it will push you forward to meet them. In this way, Rhyolite may bring you what you actually need, not what you think you need or want. In order for us to meet our goals, we sometimes have to change in order for the progress to take place. Many of us do not like to leave the comfort of change, use Rhyolite to help you realize that in order to grow we sometimes have to change. This is a stone of resolution.

Use Rhyolite during meditation to help you remember why you are here at this time, while it facilitates a calm mental state. A stone of shamans, Rhyolite can be used for astral travel and for channeling totem animals or elemental work. It is specially attuned to cats both big and small and is one of the best stones for telepathic communication with cats.

Meditation with Rhyolite

Begin by sitting comfortably with your eyes closed.

As you breath slowly in and out, let your troubles go.

Let your worries of the day out through your toes, through your fingertips.

Let your worries simply drip away, flowing out through your ears and your mouth, from your heart and your head. Let everything go.

Now relax. Feel your muscles relax and release. Unclench all the muscles in your calves, up through your hamstrings, to your lower back and your shoulders. Let your eyelids droop, your shoulders drop, and your biceps release. Feel your body surrounded by the light of day, the warm glow of the sun. Bring that light deep into your body, feel it filling up your heart and lungs, radiating down through your solar plexus and throughout your entire being.

See this light begin to pulsate with beautiful glowing shimmers of yellow, gold and pink. Allow this light to grow and radiate into the room, to touch and mingle with the light of the people sitting next to you, growing and blending, creating a light that mirrors the power of source itself. Glow. Glow and be healed. Glow and be one with the light of the Universe.

Now see this light begin to coalesce in the center of the room, building and growing into the Deva of our stone this evening. The greater consciousness that is Birds Eye Rhyolite is here to speak with us tonight. Listen, and collect your messages for yourself and for the group tonight, for all we receive is to be shared tonight. All pieces of this stone are one and the same, connected with the all that is. One can be used in place of the whole.

We are blessed. We are radiant. We are love, and we are light. Slowly gather your light back into your auric body, into the energetic envelope of your physical being. See your body bathed in light which heals your cells and returns your physical self to a state of perfect youth-full health and well-being.

You are blessed.

Return.

Cavansite

"Behold the light of source. We carry the spark that illuminates your physical reality. We are the vibration of the atom, the movement in the space, the current of your soul. What do you want to create? What do you want to de-manifest? We can help you with that. We help you invest your thoughts with the full energy they need to express themselves in the physical, and we can also help you dis-mantle unwanted thoughtforms such as dis-ease and poverty. Time is shifting on your planet, and manifestation is becoming more immediate. There is a learning curve with this process, and we are here to help you grow into this new reality with grace and ease. We will help you connect your creative expression and potential to your true voice, your soul voice."

First discovered in 1967 in Oregon, Cavansite is a rare calcium vanadium silicate (note how it is named after its chemical composition) found primarily in India, with deposits also occurring in New Zealand and Brazil. It occurs mostly in igneous locations with basalt and zeolite minerals.

Cavansite is a loving, gentle stone that helps people see their way clearly through times of change and upheaval. It helps us see the creative potential in every situation, and manifest the change we want to see in the world. It's a wonderful stone to use in meditation as it connects your third eye and throat chakras, linking you to your higher self so you can receive messages and guidance more clearly. Cavansite can aid with clear thinking and clear speaking. Many find that it also helps with dreaming, and some like to use it as a sleep aid.

It helps you see your inner truth, and resolve karmic issues. Physically, it works with the eyes and ears, and realigns your etheric blueprint to its original state – stimulating cellular healing and renewal.

Meditation with Cavansite

Relax. Feel your throat and jaw relaxing as you breathe out, your lungs expanding with joy as you breathe in.

You breathe out and your worries leave you.

You breathe in and you are filled with peace.

All is Well.

Peaceful blue light surrounds you, fills you. Your stone pulses in your hands, connecting you with the serenity and synergy of Source energy. You are connected with your true self. You at one, and you are at peace. Your stone is here to work with you synergistically, to help you reach your full creative potential so that you can fulfill your current life mission. Breathe in with your stone, and know that all is well. Take some time now to connect more fully with your stone, to receive any messages it has for you.

***

OK, now gather in your energy, bring yourself back to earth, back into your body, back into this room, into your chair, into your body. Breathe in. And Breathe out. Thank the stones. Breathe in. And Breathe out.

All is well.

Return.

Celestobarite

"Celestobarite is the perfect stone for you to start this new, paradigm shifting year. It will help you, and thus all who come in contact with you, raise your vibration and release all your fears forever. Yes, that's right, we said forever. Celestobarite is an extremely powerful yet relatively gentle tool that shows you exactly what is remaining in your way as an obstacle to your spiritual development, and allows you to move past these obstacles with ease and contentment. And the energetic effects of this stone become permanently lodged in your aura, so that everyone who comes near you also begins to feel a similar shift, and then this energy remains imprinted in them, affecting others, and so on, and so on. In this way, your small group is going to literally shift the entire world. Are you ready? There is no pressure here – all will be easy and well. You shall experience contentment and a joyful flow to your life as never before. Here we go!"

Celestobarite is a barium-rich form of Barite, or Strontium Sulphate. The well known Celestite has the same structure as Barite ($BaSO_4$), and celestobarite actually combines both Barite and Celestite crystalline properties.

Barite is used by some Native Americans in their ceremonial practices. They used it to go from physical matter to the spiritual plane. Barite leads initiative to pursue one's goals and dreams. Barite enhances friendship, harmony, and love. Release of trapped emotions. Barite has a very strong effect on and is beneficial to the psyche. It is used to assist in psychological issues, particularly obsessive-compulsive behavior, neurosis as well as agoraphobia and obsessive cleaning. Barite has a strong grounding quality that assists in matters of money and finance. It does this by clearing obstacles in one's path and strengthening your resolve. It assists those who may have a very polarized idea about money (it's never enough... or you have run up too much debt). It allows us to see the "middle ground" and to find balance in our way of thinking. On a physical level, Barite is used to cleanse the system of toxins, to soothe a nervous stomach and to assist in the healing of addictions. In the 20th century scientists discovered that barite (barium) could protect against dangerous x-rays, radioactivity and ultraviolet radiation. Barite's protective properties help those working around computers and those working around low levels of radiation.

Celestine (aka Celestite) is an Angelic stone. Celestite is used in meditation, to reach a deeper level and to move through and past fear and worry. It is used to enhance creativity and comprehension, and is therefore good when faced with a problem that needs solving. Celestite has been said to cleanse the aura and the chakras.

Meditation with Celestobarite

Imagine you hold the stone gently over your abdomen and close your eyes. Relax, and let your worries go. Relax, and breathe slowly, easily. Allow your thoughts to slowly drift away. Breathe in, and breathe out. Let your thoughts go.

Imagine a small sphere of peach and blue light emanating from your stone, creating a sphere of light that glows within your hands. See this beautiful light grow and surround you. See this light mingling with your energy, see it expanding and connecting with the light from the others in this room, growing and connecting until the entire room is bathed in this gentle, healing light.

We are all connected. We are all one. All avenues are open to you, all possible paths are strewn with light. You are blessed in all that you do.

Sit with your stone and experience the love that it holds for you. Allow you vibration to lift and raise. You are filled with light. Celestobarite is available for you, to ease you path with feelings of joy and comfort, and help you find you way. Commune now with your stone and see what particular instructions or messages it may have for you.

Now, let's begin to gather in our energies. See the light which surrounds you slowly gathering itself inward, diminishing in size but not in strength or light. See the light coat your aura, your body, with a seamless glittering light. See your true self glowing and radiating, quietly happy, easy and joyful.

You are blessed. You are a radiant being.

Feel the physical weight of your stone in your hands, and know that it is here for you, now and forever, lighting your way. And when you are ready, open you are eyes.

Charoite

"Charoite reaches a place of deep magic within you, and calls it forth. It aligns your self here, your manifestation in the physical world of the Earth-sphere, with all the creative capabilities of your true soul. It allows you to begin creating what you call magic, or miracles, here in the Earth-Sphere. It makes it easier for you to call forth your intention and mingle it with true power. You will feel calmer, yet bolder and more fulfilled, when charoite begins to speak to you."

Charoite was discovered in Russia in 1947, in the Murun mountain range near the Chara River, where it gets its name from. The gorgeous lavender limestone-based mineral comes in massively-formed deposits and generally has inclusions of feldspar (clear or white) and augite (black). Since its introduction to Western markets in 1978, it has still not been found in any other location, making this a very rare mineral.

Charoite is believed to hold great transformative powers, helping transmute negative energy and raise the vibration of those who work with it. Because of its black and white inclusions, it connects us more easily both to Earth and Spirit. Native Mongols make a tea from the stone on ceremonial days, believing the tea blesses the family protects them from evil spirits. It can also be helpful with ADD, increasing powers of concentration and memory.

As a purple stone, it aids the third eye chakra and enhances psychic development and work, as well as creativity. It has a calming, strengthening nature, encouraging feelings of safety and courage so that one can move forward in any situation. It is a very helpful stone to use during times of transition or turmoil. It is wonderful for children who are afraid of the dark, suffer from nightmares or simply resist going to sleep.

Physically, charoite is used to benefit the nervous system, eyes, head and ears. It is also believed to help shield the body from radiation. Used as a crystal elixir, it can boost detoxification processes and aid addiction rehabilitation.

Meditation with Charoite

Get comfortable. Relax.

Close your eyes and visualize a delicate purple light emanating from your third eye, swirling outwards, in front of you.

See the light pooling and forming a beautiful, fully formed, lavender lotus flower. The lotus flower is open and welcoming, and the light continues to emanate from your third eye, the lotus glows and grows, growing in size until it is large enough for you to stand on, large enough for you to walk into and sit down in the center. You walk into the center and seat yourself comfortably here, safely nestled in the heart of the lotus.

Now feel yourself opening to Charoite, much like the lotus has opened to you. Open yourself to communication from the stone. Charoite welcomes you. It has messages for you. Let us sit now, at peace within our circle of flowers, as we commune with our stones.

Now, thank your stone for the time it has spent with you. You have great work to do together in the coming months! Spend a moment now enjoying your flower, thanking it and feeling the comfort and life-energy that it has offered you.

Stand from your flower, stepping off from its petals, and see the flower get smaller and smaller, until you can reach out and hold it in your hand with your stone. Tuck your stone into the center of the flower. The energy of the lotus will forever protect and empower your stone whenever you are not working with it. Carry them with you, now, back into the room, back into your body, and RETURN!

Chlorite and Amphibole
Phantom Quartz

"We are green and white and love-Green for the heart, white for the Angels...the Angels of healing and love-We heal all things we are near-We give energy hugs because hugs are so wonderful-Companionship, love, joy in one's self and others-Relationship builders-Get rid of old relationship matters and move on no matter what type-We are here for love, we speak and work for love-Expand your heart and grow happiness with it-Love the small things in life. The small little joys, the gentle moments-The small joys will become larger & larger when you expand your heart-Most people don't realize how closed their hearts are-Society does that to us...don't trust this person, or be wary of that-In the higher realms there is no reason for fear-We are all moving towards the higher realms-Rejoice in your being and the journey you're on-What reason do you have not to?-There is no place for fear and discontent in the higher realms-Get rid of it, don't dwell on it, and it will cease to exist-You CAN create your own happiness-We help you move closer to that ability-We all have it, we help you find where you put it-We are done, thank you."

Amphibole Quartz is a rare and much sought after healing crystal containing Tremolite, Actinolite, Hornblende, Rebeckite, Richterite, Lithium and Hematite or some combination of these minerals. These very rare crystals are usually found in Minas Gerias, Brazil. Mostly seen as Beautiful Phantoms inside the quartz, they have a wonderful powerful energy and are said to put you in touch with Angelic realms. A joyous crystal carrying it or wearing bring joy and light into your life. They can awaken you to your Divinity, your Third eye and Crown Chakra. Releases worry fear and anxiety. Use to help communicate with your guardian Angel. Great for remembering your dreams, place underneath your pillow can even foster good insightful ones. Use with the other Angelic crystals (Angelite, Celestite, Seraphinite, Azeztulite, Phenacite, Angel Opal) and their combined energy is amazing! Being around these wonderful crystals can influence the way you perceive the world, actions come more from the heart, and the special energy can transform anyone near them.They help to pull out what does not belong from the system. They are said to also shield one from the abrasiveness of others. This is especially healing from those who are or have been emotionally or verbally abused. Because Amphibole Phantom Quartz stimulates the third eye and crown chakras, it is considered to be useful for connecting to the higher-self, for astral travel, to promote lucid dreaming and to facilitate interdimensional communication.

Chlorite is very positive and powerful and most favorable for healing. It is a purifier and a cleanser for the aura, chakras and meridians. Chlorite is used to counteract hostility, anger and exasperation by dissipating the energy. It is helpful in eliminating toxins and miasms from the body – drink lots of water when you use this crystal to support your detoxification process! Because of these properties it may help one to lose weight and to stimulate the production of beneficial bacteria in the body. Metaphysically chlorite can assist one is connecting with the angelic realm and to open the crown charka to healing energies from the spirit realm. Used at the heart chakra chlorite will cleanse, protect and connect you with love.

Meditation with Chlorite and Amphibole Phantom Quartz

To Meditate with this stone, use a quiet rattle, and sit quietly.

Let the sound of the rattle lift your soul from your body and up into the higher angelic realms, where you will receive messages from the guides associated with the stone.

Chlorite Hematoid Quartz

"We are clarity and insight. We help you cut away that whit you don't need with decisiveness. Hold us, you will see. Hold on, and you will let go."

These powerful hematite and chlorite included natural quartz wands are perfect for performing deep inner healing. Many have phantoms, and all are included with both minerals.

Chlorite is very positive and powerful and most favorable for healing. It is a purifier and a cleanser for the aura, chakras and meridians. Chlorite is used to counteract hostility, anger and exasperation by dissipating the energy. It is helpful in eliminating toxins and miasms from the body – drink lots of water when you use this crystal to support your detoxification process! Because of these properties it may help one to lose weight and to stimulate the production of beneficial bacteria in the body. Metaphysically chlorite can assist one is connecting with the angelic realm and to open the crown charka to healing energies from the spirit realm. Used at the heart chakra chlorite will cleanse, protect and connect you with love.

Red Hematite in quartz is called hematoid quartz. It has significant grounding and balance properties, allowing the quartz to do intense work without destabilizing or causing discomfort to the subject. This is especially beneficial when blended with chlorite, helping one get to the true core of physical, mental and spiritual dis-ease with ease. Healing takes place more rapidly, and more comfortably. It is a great crystal to use during the ascension process, as we let go of that which no longer serves our highest good and shift into higher frequencies.

Additionally, phantoms help us release the past and process old issues, so that we can truly transcend and grow through the life experience. Chlorite phantoms are especially wonderful at helping us ground and tap into the Earth's living matrix for healing while all this inner work is going on.

Meditation with Chlorite Hematoid Quartz

Breathe in. Breathe out.

Hold your stone and as you breathe out, imagine that all the toxins you exhale flow through the crystal, transmuted. As you breathe in, take in the fresh, clean energy of the earth deep into you. The longer you do this, the more refreshed and clear you feel.

Breathe in. Breathe out.

Now I want you to imagine that you can see the divine web of mass consciousness that flows through all life on this planet. You can see the Earth's living matrix weaving through this room, connecting you with everyone, and everything. Connecting you to all of nature. Connecting you to your divine blueprint. Connecting you to source as it is meant to be channeled into the physical on this planet.

Breathe in, and connect to the living matrix. Breathe in, and feel the energy of the Earth, of purified Source energy, reenergizing you and making you whole. Pure. As you were meant to be. Breathe in. And Breathe out.

Now turn your attention to your stone. In your mind's eye, you gaze deeply into your stone, and you see an entire forest within. You enter that forest, where the spirit of your stone awaits. You enter the forest, and you speak with your stone. Now is the time to connect fully, express what it is you are hoping for and what you would like to transcend, and then listen to your stone as it tells you what is actually going on, and what is meant to be. Listen to your stone, as it shares the messages of the matrix with you.

***

Now thank the spirit of your stone, say a prayer of gratitude and blessing for all of the Earth's living matrix, and untwine yourself from your vision.

Breathe in. Breathe out.

And return.

Chrysocolla

"We open the door. We let in the light. We help you heal your self, we are the physician's stone, a stone of regeneration and energy. We activate the thymus gland and remind your body that it can live forever. You can live forever. This is real. This is the ability of your human body, to live and experience as long as you wanting and desiring to live and to be in this vessel. So often, you choose to begin anew, to begin fresh, forgetting that your body has the potential to refresh itself. You do not need to be reborn. You have the power to rebirth your self here, now. This is the truth, for we are the truth bearers."

Chrysocolla is a copper silicate with gorgeous green-blue hues. It is often found with quartz, and when tumbled reminds many people of the planet Earth viewed from outer space. Come people call it the "Peace Crystal" due to its ability to calm and soothe the mind. Chrysocolla is a gentle stone, unleashing its healing powers upon the powers slowly so that your psyche and physical body can acclimate smoothly to its healing powers. Due to its copper content, Chrysocolla is a wonderful stone for channeling energies and cleaning the aura, releasing toxic emotions and stress from all layers of the body. It helps you reach into your inner well of strength and fortitude.

Chrysocolla is very stabilizing and fortifying, and a wonderful stone to use around the home or office to improve communication and relationships. Place it in upon your altar to help you attract a mate or lover. Some people like to combine it with copper wrapping to further increase Chrysocolla's abilities. It is also believed by many to help foster wealth and increase good fortune.

Native American shamans used Chrysocolla to boost the immune system and soothe patients. Indeed, it is known to help benefit rational, clear thinking, and is often used by public speakers boost confidence. Crystal healers place Chrysocolla directly on body to lower blood pressure; treat infections, fever, and pain; and detoxify the liver.

Pure Chrysocolla is a very soft stone, so it is not always easy to work with in jewelry settings. Most jewelry pieces you find use chrysocolla in a druzy form or combined with quartz.

Due to its high copper content, chrysocolla is best infused in elixirs via the indirect method.

Meditation with Chrysocolla

Let's all breathe out. Let your breath naturally return to your body, just focus on breathing out, and then allowing your body to return to its natural, breathe-filled state.

Breathe out the worries of the day.

Breathe out the toxins you've accumulated.

Breathe out the thoughts from yesterday.

Breathe out.

Breathe out.

There, doesn't that feel good? Do you feel how naturally light and easy you are? Do you feel how calm and serene you can be?

Now, let's work with Chrysocolla. Imagine the stone at your thymus gland, and allow the energy of the stone to grow and expand with you. Breathe out, exhaling the used breath, and breathe in the pure flowing energy of the chrysocolla. Feel your heart center and your thymus energies expanding. Feel your endocrine system flowing. Your blood, glowing. Your synapsis connected, clicking into place, expanding and being in a perfect state of alignment. Fell the wonder that is the perfect vehicle of you – your body.

Align with your stone and feel the connection on a cellular level. Allow it to connect to your mind, your thoughts. Your voice, its voice. Its voice, your voice.

You hear it, it hears you. What has it to say to you? Listen.

Continue to breath, out, and in, and know that you can not lose this feeling of connection. It is with you, for you, within you, of you, always.

Always you are connected.

Always.

Return.

Corundum

"We are the foundation of love on your planet. We harmonize all the races, regulate the flow of energy between the sexes, between the masculine and the feminine, we bring peace to all people. When we are beautiful we are valued, but we should all be valued, for we all hold the key to your inner peace, which brings outer peace, joy and harmony on earth for all beings. And when we say all beings we mean ALL beings – all rocks, all trees, all animals, all people, all dirt, all earth, all devas all ALL. All is beautiful and right. All is what it is meant to be. All is as all should be. Do not fight for harmony. Just let it come to you, let it in, let it flow. Let it BE."

Corundum forms as a naturally transparent crystal of aluminum oxide. Various colors come from inclusions of titanium, iron and chromium. Gem quality corundum is highly transparent and known as ruby (red), padparadscha (pink-orange) and sapphire (green, blue and all other color varieties). The corundum we are working with today comes to us from Madagascar, but it can be found throughout the world – corundum used in emery boards is found in Peeksill, NY. Look on beaches and stream beds – some varieties of "mica" is actually corundum. Corundum is incredibly hard, 9.0 on the Mohs scale, and can scratch almost every mineral and will sometimes glow under UV light. Some corundum is very color stable, while others can fade quickly in direct sunlight, even within a matter of days.

Corundum raises your energy levels and spiritual vibration, so that you can reach new levels of peace and harmony. This in turn boosts manifestation and creativity, allowing your ambitions and aspirations to become realized and enhancing self-actualization. Corundum teaches you to have confidence in your self and your own intuitive guidance, so that you are better able to believe in yourself and follow your true path. It helps you release negative conceptions and old emotional baggage. It can help you have greater insight into what has been holding you back, and release old patterns of anger and irritability.

Physically, corundum is used by crystal healers to soothe skin irritations, benefit eye conditions and help the body self-harmonize, regulating detoxification and elimination functions.

Meditation with Corundum

Breathe in, and breathe out. As you breathe in, feel the air flowing through both your arms, through your legs, harmonizing both sides of your body. Feel your body in balance, the left balanced with the right, the right balanced with the left. Feel both sides flowing into each other, so that you can't tell where one half ends and one begins. Feel your lungs working together as one, neither stronger than the other, both sides working in tandem, creating a harmonious resonance between your masculine and your feminine, your left and your right. Feel how it is to be in balance.

Now, hold your stone to your solar plexus just below your ribs. Breathe out, and feel the stone awakening, accepting your energy and resonating with your own energy, so that you become as one.

Feel the power and the wisdom emanating from the stone within your own aura. What messages does your stone have for you today? How may you work together for the highest good? Does it have any particular instructions for you? Take some time now to sit and listen to your stone.

All is well. Thank your stone now, and gather in your energy. Return to the room, to your body, and be at peace.

All is well.

Return.

Creedite

"Vibrating in the same light ray as citrine, creedite connects the roots of your self-confidence and joy to your heart chakra, allowing you to truly let happiness and abundance into the core of your being and soul. This stone helps you feel more confident and strong, uplifting not only your own energy layers of being but letting your light radiate to those around you, creating harmony and bliss wherever you go. For those of you who have been working with all the stones in Maya's group, this is the stone that will help you synthesize all the past lessons of the last 6 month together, the stone you have been waiting for. After this stone, a new, heightened cycle of learning will begin."

Creedite is a rare hydrated calcium aluminum sulfate hydroxide fluoride mineral and is a product of the intense oxidation of ore. It was first discovered in 1916 in the Creed Quadrangle in Mineral City, Colorado. It forms white, colorless orange to purple crystals. Orange Creedites usually form spiny porcupine-like rounds with bristly crystals protruding in every direction.

Creedite aligns the upper chakras allowing for clarity in expression of the spiritual realm. This is a high vibration mineral, it creates an happy or euphoric energy ! This in turn allows for total relaxation and surrender allowing one to clearly receive information during meditation. Creedite enhances spirituality and is a tool to be used in channeling meditation to provide clarity in the verbalization of the message which is transmitted. Creedite helps provide a driving force. Is used for the simulation of vitamin A, E and B also used to cleanes the liver and regulate the heartbeat.

It can assist in the expansion of awareness and feelings of upliftment. It can enhance meditation, helping to release any blockages in the upper chakras. Creedite is a stone of the Light and can help one manifest that light in one's everyday life. Creedite will assist in bringing into form that which comes from the deep awareness that it also brings forth. Orange Creedites can stimulate creative vision and are excellent for raising the vibration of work space.

Creedite helps the user to attune to a higher spiritual vibration and clarify the channeled messages received. Creedite also helps to gain access to the sacred texts, and to understand the subtle messages within. Use Creedite when working with astral travel or out of body experiences. Creedite will act as a guide during the event and will help to recall the experiences of the event.

It helps us to be connected to the spiritual opening. Beneficial to the body's cleansing system. Yellow/orange creedite has hematite inclusions in it and is useful for blood detoxification. Helps one discover how best to express themselves and intuitively understand other eye, crown, etheric chakras. Light body. Creedite is often found with fluorite as it uses the fluorite to grow out of.

Caution: It is not recommended to use this directly in the creation of an elixir as it contains Aluminum.

Meditation with Creedite

Breathe in.

Breathe out.

Feel the clean air entering your body through your mouth, entering your lungs, filling you will pure, clear energy.

Breathe in the purity.

Feel the air cleansing every cell in your body, feel the air pulsing through you, into every cell, in and out your skin through osmosis, in and out.

Clean. Clear. Alive.

Now visualize a small tangerine ball of energy glowing in front of you. See the ball grow larger, now the size of a grapefruit, now the size of a soccer ball. Growing larger and larger, brighter and more beautiful. Now reach out, hold that ball of light in your hands, and bring it over you, into you. See the light seated in your chest, glowing, radiating, filling your entire being with pure golden light.

Now see your Creedite in front of you, also glowing, also radiating pure, joyful energy, and hold it in your hands. Let yourself dialogue with the stone, feel how it would like you to use it best to enhance your learning and physical incarnation in this life. Sit with the stone for awhile, and allow yourself to become familiar with each other.

Now gently gather your radiance into your body, enfolding the light within your being. Release your meditation.

You are blessed, you are whole.

Danburite

"We refresh your soul, washing away fear and insecurity, and flood it with pure love. Not the sort of love you earthlings are so familiar with, but the truest, purest, loving and angelic vibration of SOURCE. Once you are in that feeling, it is easy for you to remember that there are no mistakes, that you have chosen every aspect of your being and of your reality, and that you are here on purpose. You chose your families on purpose. You chose your bodies and genetics on purpose. You chose your life on purpose. Everything is happening as it should, whether you feel you've made mistakes or nor. You are in the right place, at the right time, doing the right thing."

First discovered in Danbury, CT, Danburite is relatively common calcium borosilicate that forms rectangular prisms with a diamond-like wedge face and striated sides. It is found in large quantities in Mexico, Bolivia and Russia. All danburite is extremely calming and soothing, with the pink pieces having the strongest peaceful, loving vibration and a strong connection to the angelic realms.

Danburite activates the heart and crown chakras, allowing the transmission and reception of positive frequencies from higher levels of Source. Although it activates mental activity and upper chakras, it keeps us in our bodies, connected to the here and now so that we can integrate these beneficial energies with our physical experience. Whether we spend too much time in our upper chakras and out of our bodies, or our souls are still not sure that incarnating was the best idea, danburite helps us feel more comfortable in our bodies and brings us back to reality while facilitating an open channel to our higher selves.

Try danburite by your bed or under your pillow to experience clearer dreams, or in meditation to help you understand your true path.

Meditation with Danburite

Breathe in, and breathe out. Relax your mind. Allow your shoulders to roll back down into a relaxed position. Feel your lungs easing and opening with each breath out.

Breathe out, and feel your heart opening, feel yourself opening to receive wisdom and light from your stone.

Relax, and imagine your crystal at your heart center. Visualize pink light surrounding you, flowing in and out of your heart, out of all your pores. As your heart continues to expand and open, a white ball of light appears over your head, getting larger and brighter as you breathe in, and out. Your heart center is wide open, and the white light begins to stream down into your crown chakra, down into your body through the top of your head, filling your heart center and radiating out through your entire body. You are filled with light. You are a radiant being. The light begins to glow through your skin, through your pores and your mouth and your ears. You are filled with light, and you feel wonderful. Refreshed. Comfortable and alive.

Your crystal is ready to talk with you now. Take some time to listen to your stone, receive the messages it brings from the higher realms, and find out how it would like to be used over the coming month...

All is well. The light that fills you begins to slowly dim, storing itself in all your cells and organs for whenever you need it. The light is your birthright. You can access it at any time, over and over again, whenever you reach for it. Remember that you are the light.

All is well.

You are the light.

Return.

Dunite
(Olivine Peridotite)

"Dunite is in the family of Peridot, but it carries a slightly different vibration. It allows the energy centers of the solar plexus and third chakras to merge and flow with ease into the heart center. It brings in more protection and grounding energy than the more commonly used peridot, thus allowing for fuller, more complete feelings of forgiveness and closure with past issues where blame, anger and guilt have been stored in the lower chakras. Dunite allows these issues to rise to the surface and be transmuted by the light of love."

Dunite will cleanse and stimulate the heart and solar plexus chakras, fostering openness and acceptance in relationships. It provides a shield of protection around the body, and should be removed whenever you are needing to balance or cleanse the physical body or any chakras, as it will block energy work on any unrelated chakras. Replace the dunite when you are through, and it will help you maintain the balance you have created.

It helps to mend bruised egos by lessening anger, guilt, obsessions or jealousy, helping one find delight and happiness in ones life. It will magnify the inner aspects of any circumstance or situation. It furthers the understanding of changes which are occurring in your life, and helps you identify patterns which may be impeding your growth. If you have done the psychological work, you will move forward even faster while it helps you understand your destiny and spiritual purpose and release old burdens and baggage.

Olivine helps boost confidence and assertiveness without aggression. It helps you admit mistakes and move on, and can greatly improve difficult relationships.

It can be used to find things which are lost, whether they be of the spirit or the physical.

In the physical, try using Dunite to improve your vision, digestion, circulation and heart. It acts as a general tonic, reeasing toxins, and strengthening and regenerating the body. Emotionally, it relieves stress and is helpful for bipolar disorder.

Meditation with Dunite

Hold your stone at your solar plexus and close your eyes.

Relax.

Feel the beat of your heart releasing your stress, your fear, your day.

Let it all go, and feel each beat of your heart cleaning your body,

increasing the flow of love through

your lungs,

your stomach,

your liver,

your hips,

your shoulders,

your thighs,

your arms,

your head, your knees,

your feet,

your toes.

Just relax.

Hold your stone and allow it work with your body to bring you to perfection. Ask for its help in protecting your energies, in clearing away old hurts and fear, in perfecting your chakras and aligning your heart and soul with your destiny here and now. Does it have any messages for you? Open your heart and your mind, and let it all flow.

You are blessed. You are perfection.

Thank your stone, and begin your return to your body, to this room.

BE here now. Return, and open your eyes. Welcome back!

Elimia Agate

"Bursting with energy and dynamism, you couldn't ask for a better team of co-workers than us! Use us to empower all your intentions. Grids are significantly amped up by our inclusion. Circulation and metabolism is increased. Energy is manifest. We are life, we are energy. We love to work, and we love to race!"

Elimia Agate (aka Turritella Agate) is a fossiliferous agate found in Wyoming in the Green River Formation. Volcanic mineral analysis of Green River Formation artifacts indicate that the fossils date from approximately 50 million years ago, during the Eocene epoch. The rock's most popular name, Turritella Agate, is a misnomer, because the fossils are not that of the saltwater turritella snail family, but are from freshwater snails called Elimia tenera. Still the name persists in most circles.

Formed in the large sedimentary basins of lakes, Elimia is considered a very wise, protective and shielding stone that helps anchor one in eth present and boost powers of concentration and skills. It is most commonly used to access past wisdom, the knowledge of our ancestors and past lives, because it helps reconcile the past with the present.

Physically, it has always been considered by shamans and elders to be a strong, healing stone with powerful medicine. It can revitalize and cleanse dense energy both in living, organic beings and in the earth itself. It is a great stone for enhancing grid and prayer work. Its strong energies are particularly well-suited to distance healing.

A traveler's stone, both vehicular and out of body.

Meditation with Elimia

For this meditation, imagine that you sit within a circle of elimia stones, and you hold one in your hand.

Breathe deeply, centering your mind and body. Feel how you are the anchor, how you are the pull on the energy of source. You anchor the world. You anchor your reality. Energy pulses into you, through you. Creating you. Lighting you up. Clarifying you. Building you. Releasing you. Over and over again, every moment of the day, as you breathe in, and breathe out.

Feel yourself flowing with vitality, flowing with crisp, clear energy. You are pure. You are light.

Elimia is here to help you. Right now, it is purifying your physical vessel, getting it ready for the mental and spiritual tasks you have set for your self. How can you an Elimia work most competently together? How can it aid you? Spend some time now with your stones and see what you can accomplish together as we begin this new year.

...

Now, breathe in, and breathe out. Relax. Thank your stones, and spend some time envisioning the best outcomes for what you have talked about this evening.

That's it. Yes. Relax, and open to the new blessings that are coming your way.

Breathe out, knowing that you are creating your reality.

Breathe in, knowing that you are drawing it to you.

All is well. You are blessed.

Return.

Emerald

"We are the lightworkers of the crystal world, the healers of the heart, the ones who open the body to all the energies of the soul. Wear us, and you will be infused with the power of source. Wear us, and feel the fullness of your momentum and capacity for creation. You are a powerhouse. We supply the fuel, we tune up your engine, we rev you up. Tap in to the green ray of light healing, and reconnect with love, wonder and joy."

Emeralds are a variety of beryl whose color derives from chromium. It is a very hard stone, making it rather difficult to cut. In jewelry, the best settings will protect the stone from chipping. As a green stone, emerald is connected to the heart chakra and considered a "stone of love". In Asia it is associated with Quan Yin, the goddess of compassion and mercy. In Rome it was associated with Mercury, the God of messages and travel, and was carried travelers for protection. Early Christians wore it to show their faith and belief.

Emerald has a long history of use for healing and protection. It was carried in workshops by ancient artisans to improve their eyesight, placed over the heart to protect one from demonic possession, and believed to heal digestive disorders. Modern crystal healers use emerald to open the heart chakra and improve a variety of mood and stress disorders, as well as treat pain and back issues. Emeralds are extremely powerful, high vibration stones. They soothe the nervous system while strengthening and invigorating the body.

Emeralds can vary in coloration. The blue-green emeralds are considered more Yin, while the warmer yellow-greens are more yang. Light green emeralds are considered the most highly attuned with psychic, spiritual matters, and darker emeralds are believed to be more calming and physically healing. To recharge your stone, wash it with cool water and place near a ruby, quartz or diamond.

As with all green stones, emeralds can be used to encourage growth, fertility and abundance. This may be applied to the home, work, garden or one's own body. It is cooling, and may be helpful placed near those with traumatic injuries or burns. Try making a gem elixir of this stone with water to soothe eyestrain, treat pain and promote general healing and immunity.

Meditation with Emerald

Close your eyes and get comfortable. Breathe in the clear, fresh air of the evening and relax. Feel yourself becoming lighter, more open and free, with every breath you take. Breathe in, and feel yourself getting lighter. Breathe out, and feel yourself releasing heavy thoughts and dramas. In with the light. Out with the drama.

In.

And out.

Now, I'd like you to see yourself surrounded by greenery. You are warm, and all around you are gorgeous green leaves, a rainforest of leaves filled with delicate aromas and soft noises. It is warm and humid. You are relaxed and comfortable. Everything feels easy and open here. Welcoming.

You sit in this forest and you feel good. It is sunny high above the leafy canopy, but here you are bathed in the green light of the forest, your skin is kissed by the warm mist of the air, and you feel happy. Free. Easy. Comfortable.

On the ground in front of you, there is a large emerald, the mother emerald from which all your emeralds came. It is glowing. Speaking.

Sit now, with your emeralds and the mother emerald, and listen to her message. Let your stones be rejuvenated by her light. Let your healing begin with her voice.

All is well. Thank the mother stone now for her lesson. Thank the forest for its canopy and the blessed oxygen it feeds the planet. Take a deep breath in, and a big breath out.

Return now, and let the healing begin!

Epidote

"Epidote will bring you the balance and serenity which so many are seeking. It helps you cool off tempers while strengthening your inner resources. A still river, it's waters run deep: do not underestimate the power of epidote to carry you to new and exciting places in a short amount of time, safely and surely, it will deliver you."

Epidote is a basic calcium, aluminum, iron silicate.

Epidote is a stone of increase. It has a tendency to increase anything it touches, whether the thing it touches is energy or a material object. It is a stone that enhances emotional and spiritual growth. It cleanses repressed emotions once and for all.

Epidote opens those who have refused their spiritual growth. Clears the emotional body aura. Cleanses old repressed emotions once and for all. *Those drawn to this stone are being shaken into spiritual awakening by healing the linkage between us and the psychic plane. It helps us to receive certain knowledge often from firsthand sources. Enhances perception and personal power. Excellent for attunement in all aspects of awareness, improvement, abundance, and healing.

Some like to use Epidote to help them through times of difficulty, it dissolves sadness, sorrow, self-pity and grief. It is very good at stopping panic attacks. Epidote also clears the emotional body aura. It stimulates perception, participation and interaction as well as personal power. It also dispels critcalness and closed-mindedness. Epidote is also said to promote patience. Epidote can inject a sense of hopeful optimism into one's emotional body, helping to bring the mind into a higher vibration. Crystal healers like to work with Epidote for its ability to clear congestion and energy blockages in the physical and subtle bodies. Epidote will help to balance and stabilize the energy flow in the body. Epidote is also used to help dissipate tumors by releasing stagnant energies in the area.

In the physical realm, it's simple grounding 'back to the Earth' vibration supports all healing processes. It can be used as a digestive aid, especially for those who have a hard time assimilating food intake. It tells us when we need to eat better and when we need to rest. Epidote increases personal power, clears the emotional body aura, and even increases memory, making it a helpful when looking for lost object.

Fun Fact: The green color found in Unakite is in fact inclusions of Epidote

Meditation with Epidote

Relax. Be quiet.

Be still.

Let your mind be at peace with itself.

Breathe in, and out, and let each breath lighten your body, lifting you higher, and higher, up into the clouds, above the mountains. See the warm glow of the sunset bathing you with its glow. You are warm and secure, safe and filled with a feeling of ease.

Epidote carries the green ray of healing within, the light of the sun. Feel this light healing you, lifting you, soothing you.

The spirit of Epidote is with you now. What would you like to ask it? All questions are yours, all answers are here. How shall you work with this stone, does it have a particular name or a message for you?

Let the messages of Epidote sit with you. Let the light of the stone, the light of source, the joy of the sun, stay with you as you slowly sink back to Earth, back into your body.

You are blessed. You are whole.

Return.

Eudialyte

"Eudialyte is stone that allows you to GROW. It releases your fears which hold you back, and your fear of fears, too. It helps to ground your desires in reality and bring them to fruition in a balanced manner that blends joyful creation with logic and mass consciousness. It helps you to rationalize everything you want in a way that helps you to attain it more quickly and fully."

Eudialyte is considered a personal power stone that increases and revitalizes one's personal power. Eudialyte helps with clairaudience, manifestation, and psychic resonance and abilities, and is a psychically protective stone. It is sometimes considered a "fine tuner". Eudialyte is also a stone of the heart, bringing harmony of heart matters, and dispelling jealousy. As eudialyte combines pink and red, it also brings the root and heart chakras into alignment, as well as activating the heart chakra. It activates the Alpha brain wave pattern during the creative state as well as the dream state. Emotionally it is helpful for learning to trust oneself and others, and eases compulsive behavior and thinking. It infuses the being with inspiration and confidence.

Physically, eudialyte is good for healing the emotions, increasing vitality, eye problems, pancreas, thyroid, and purifying the blood. It has also been used as a very accurate diagnostic tool. It opens the Kundalini with energy flowing from the crown to the base chakra, opening the chakra centers and allowing a clear pathway for the movement of the Kundalini.

The color really is one of its most distinctive features. This too gives the clues as to its properties ... the root and the heart chakras, linking them energetically to unite compassion and love with a non-judgmental attitude, allowing one to then "see" from the heart. Eudialyte is a personal power stone, deepening the ability to act appropriately regarding issues of power between people.

It is also a powerfully energetic stone and said to be able to clear the space of entities that have not been able to pass on after death. For those working with the terminally ill this stone is especially useful. Among the ancients it has also been known as the "stone of Hyacinthuys", one which dispels jealousy and rings the "bell" in ones mind and in ones heart whenever soul-travelers reunite.

Meditation with Eudialyte

To connect with Eudialyte, a walking meditation is best. Make your way outside and take a deep breath and begin walking.

Enjoy the clear air, the sounds around you. Enjoy being on the earth. You are here for a reason, and it is good. Know that all is well.

Think of Eudialyte, connecting with its rich raspberry flecks, black and white inclusions, and know that you walk in balance through life. You are on the right path. As you walk, let your mind wander and trust eudialyte to help you connect with the synchronicity and harmony of Source, of All-that-Is.

All will be well.

You are well.

Fairy Concretions

"So Old, So Slow. We were under pressure for so very,, very long. It took us a long time to become who wer are. We each hold a spark of life inside us, a small, brilliant spark that we nourished and protected through all the pressure, through everything that wore down the other life around us. We are the shields of life. We hold the spark of purity and awareness within us. We hold the memories of a better time, when humans were more alive, more pure, more elevated. We can help you return to that, we can help your DNA remember what it was, we can awaken the spark of purity and divinity within you, despite all the pressures that surround you in the world you have made.."

Fairy Concretions (aka fairy stones or harricana) are found primarily in Canada and Alaska. They formed in Quaternary glacial deposits and are now found in or near lakes left as the glaciers receded over 10,000 years ago. They are comprised primarily of calcite, formed from limestone clay under great pressure by the mile-high glaciers above them. The concretions themselves almost always have a small item within them, such as a small stone (pyrite is common), or fossilized stick, bug or leaf. I like to think of them as glacial "pearls."

The Algonquin Tribe of Canada thought these stones looked like biscuits. The Harricana river near Quebec has many fairy concretions along its shores, and its name actually means "River of the Biscuits." The Algonquins believe the stones come from the

Little People, or Fairies. They are thought to bring good luck and protection, and it was tradition to give them to loved ones as a token of affection and blessing. Carrying one on a fishing or hunting trip was believed to invoke the blessings of the Little People and ensure a good catch – these days, they continue to be associated with abundance and properity. Large ones kept in the home would protect the inhabitants from illness and bad spirits.

Fairy stones are nurturing and helpful. They love to work with humans to help them feel safe and comfortable, so that they can relax into their true nature and live joyfully. They help us release old traumas and let go of what isn't needed or beneficial in our lives. Fairy stones allow obstacles (both internal or external) to naturally dissolve out of our way.

If you want to connect to ancient knowledge and civilizations, earth knowledge or the powerful element of water, fairy stones can help with that, too. In Sweden, the stones have been found on beaches and at archeological digs and are known to locals as "marlekor" or "mallrikor". There they are often discovered with holes bored through them or cut and polished, indicating that they were valued and used there, too.

Meditation with Fairy Stone

Close your eyes and relax.

Breathe in deeply, hold for four counts, and breathe out.

Breathe in, hold, and breathe out.

Breathe in, hold, and breathe out.

Relax.

Breathe in. Breathe out.

Let go.

See the night sky, the stars are out, the moon is just as it is now, a thin crescent moon, hanging low in the sky. The Pleiades are shining and you feel comforted knowing you are being watched by the seven sisters, the elf stars. You lie back on the grass and feel relaxed. Open. Full of possibilities. Everything is going so well for you – what will you do next. You lie there, gazing up as the stars, and think about the possibilities.

***

Your fairy stone is in your hand, and you hold it up to the sky, letting it be bathed in the glow of the moon and the stars. Your fairy stone pulses with energy. It is awakened by the light, cleansed by the moon and empowered by the stars. You put it to your forehead and enjoy it's cool touch. You stone has much to say to you. Listen to your stone. Allow your stone to share its power and freedom with you.

Listen now and hear its messages, see if there is anything it wants you to do, any special way it would like you to work with it.

All is well. Your stone is happy you have chosen to work with it. It is ready to get to the work! It has been waiting for you for so very, very long.

Give your stone a kiss goodbye, and return now, back into this room, back into your chair, into your body, and get ready to do the work!

Return.

Fairy Cross - Staurolite

"We are called fairy crosses, but really we are so much more than that. Use us to connect to the fae if you wish – but we are here to connect you to the entire to earth, to all beings sentient in your dimension and beyond to who you are connected already through your energy patterning and even your DNA. We are as magnets, who will draw to you a greater connectivity with all that is, all that was, and all that will be. Use us to draw to you that which you are wanting. Be very careful – don't think about the things you do not want when you are using us, for we can not tell the difference! We merely hear your frequency, and amplify it. In all ways, for all times. We are of the universe. We are everything. We are all all all all. Use us wisely, and do not be afraid!"

Staurolite, aka "Fairy Cross", is a brown/grey crystal most often found within a mica schist. They are a combination of silica, iron and aluminum. Staurolite crystallizes at 60 or 90 degree angles, hence the stone's cross-like structure. Found only in rocks once subjected to great heat and pressure, the mineral was formed long, long ago, during the rise of mountains. Tennessee, Georgia, Virginia and Montana, USA; Brazil; Scotland, Italy and France. For many years people held these little crosses in superstitious awe, firm in the belief that they protected the wearer against witchcraft, sickness, accidents and disaster. It is well known that President Theodore Roosevelt and President Wilson, Thomas A. Edison, Colonel Charles Lindbergh, and many other historical figures including some of the crown heads of Europe carried these little stones on their person. Another legend has it that Staurolite was used to heal Richard the Lionhearted during his Crusades in the Middle East, when he suffered from malaria.

Staurolite represents the four elements and joining of spirit with earth/matter. It encourages spirituality, compassion, allowingness, dis-attachment; bringing your Focus centered on the Here and Now. This stone is said to provide a connection between the physical, astral and extra-terrestrial planes. It can provide an overpowering "release" in stressful situations and provides support, initiation and incentive in dealing with detrimental habits.

Metaphysical rock collectors, crystal healers, and Lightworkers who are conscious of their connection to the Angelic Hierarchy may especially prize Staurolite's strong connection to Archangel Michael.

Present day crystal healers have used Staurolite to ground an individual with a tendency to float away from the material world, or to be lost in abstract realms of mental reasoning. Staurolite has also been used to treat depression, fevers, addictive personality traits and symptoms of stress. Staurolite is used by healers to physically counter the effects of aging, encourage muscle and blood formation, and benefit general well being.

Meditation with Staurolite

Close your eyes and sit comfortably. Loosen your muscles. Unclench your arms, your hands, your legs, your teeth, your jaws. Roll your shoulders. Lighten the load. Release all your tension from the day. Just it all go. You can do this. You can do anything you want. Everything in the world is at your fingertips, it is all yours for the asking. Release your fears. Release your tensions. Release your anxiety.

Do you feel lighter? No? Let us call in Archangel Michael now, to assist you. We are calling upon the presence of archangel Michael to join us here tonight to help lift our spirits and wash away our fears. To fill us all with courage and vibrant energies. To strengthen our bodies and our minds. To nourish our souls with the strength of Source, of God, of all that is Good in this Universe. Here we are. Feel the light and love of the angels filling your bodies with joy and laughter, with confidence and gratitude.

You are one with all. You are one with Source. You are blessed and loved and perfect.

What would you like to be? What would you like to do? Who are you really? Reach out to your Staurolite now with all the love and joy and excitement in your heart. Let the radiance of your being connect to the stone. See the light of your soul cleansing the stone of all prior connections and contacts. See the stone filled with beautiful red and white light, washed clean and pure. See it glowing from within, radiant, warm, vibrationally aligned now with all the Source intentions of your being. Everything your soul desires, everything your higher self is wanting for you, all the happiness and joy that is due to you as a child of the Light, now your crystal is attuned to these thoughts and vibrations. Attuned only to the good in you, the light in you, the love of you.

Sit now with your stone. Allow yourself to perceive any messages it has for you, allow yourself to receive pure communications and designs.

Now release your communications. Release your intentions. Let them go, into the universe to be aligned with source for the highest good of all, for now and all time.

You are whole.

You are blessed.

Feel the warmth of Archangel Michael surround you as he returns you to this physical reality, as he accompanies you back into the everyday earthly planes.

He is with you always, whenever you need him.

The End.

Fire Agate

"Fire Agate is grounding and energizing. It brings in all the creative power of the universe to you on the powerful arc of the rainbow. It is the voice of source. It is the mind of the angels. It is the power of the earth. It is YOU. It is now, only in the now, and it will help you to find your true center."

Fire agate is said to represent absolute perfection. Fire agate can help with spiritual advancement and progression. It promotes and enhances energy, including meditation, ritual, and spiritual healing energies. It also balances masculine (active) and feminine (receptive) energies.

It instills spiritual fortitude. Fire Agate has a deep calming energy that brings, courage, protection and safety. It is a protection stone with strong grounding powers. Mystical lore says that it relieves fears, halts gossip and even reflects any threat of harm back to the source. It is also said that it can take the edge off the emotional charge of problems.

Fire agate links to the fire element and is used as an aid to improve sexual and creative activity, stimulating vitality and opening the base chakra. Fire agate is often used in spells to increase skills in communication in writing and speaking. It can also heighten creative visualization.

Hold a fire agate to inspire inner knowledge to emerge in the resolution of problems. It also helps in overcoming addictions, and other destructive desires.

Physically it heals the stomach, nervous, endocrine systems, strengthens night vision and reduces hot flashes (contrary to what one might guess!) Metaphysical healing lore professes that fire agate enhances all healing energies, and assists with healing of the circulatory system, lymph system, intestines. Fire agate is associated primarily with the sacral and root chakras.

Meditation with Fire Agate

We begin in darkness. Eyes closed, minds quiet, we breathe in the darkness.

Breathe.

No thoughts.

No sounds.

Just quiet.

You feel warm, and secure, and protected. You are connected to everything here in the darkness. You are one with all.

You feel a pleasant weight upon you, cuddled by the air around you. Your thoughts and feelings are only of joy, always of joy.

Deep in the darkness, you see a shimmer ahead of you, a tiny light that dances to and from. This makes you curious, you wonder what it could be, and no sooner do you have that thought than you hear a distant rumble, and your heart becomes exhilarated. You rush through the darkness and into the shimmering light, as the tiny dot becomes hundreds and thousands of points of light and you are surrounded by kindred spirits, all those to who you were and are connected.

You dance in the glow of each other, happy and alive. You are one with all. You are Joy-Full. You are alive.

Gather up your feelings of oneness and connection, and carry them with you as you dance back into your heart, into your mind, into your soul.

You are one.

You are whole.

You are blessed.

Flint

"We are hard, yet we are easy. We can be made into anything. We do not fret or worry when life chips away at us. We are glad to be of service, to be part of the action and flow of life. We look hard and unmoving to you, yet we hold the spark of life within us. Are you wondering what life holds in store for you? We never wonder. We know we hold all the answers and possibilities within us. As do you."

Flint, also known as chert, is a variety of cryptocrystalline quartz similar to chalcedony with a larger crystalline structure and often waxy appearance. Flint is a sedimentary rock and contains water. Struck against a piece of steel, it will give off a spark to help you light a fire.

Old carved, flint-knapped pieces were often called Elf-Shot, believed to be left over from hunting weapons of the Fae. A piece of flint worn as an amulet was believed to protect one from elves and other mystical harm. Shamans worldwide have used flint as a ceremonial tool to ward off evil and call in fire and earth energies.

Flint is considering a strengthening, protective stone. It helps boost self-esteem and cut away brain-fog and indecision, showing the way to clarity. It is a grounding stone that helps heal the root chakra while connecting us to the divine through the crown chakra, activating kundalini energy as it travels upwards through all the chakras and the spine.

Flint increases concentration and helps us to bring our dreams and desires in reality. It illuminates truth in all situations (including our own being) and encourages honest communication. As such, it also enhances spiritual growth, aligning all aspects of the self with conscious intent and purpose.

As a member of the quartz family, flint is a great overall healer of the body, including broken bones. It is used especially to help heal the detoxifying, eliminating organs of our body: the colon, liver and lungs.

Meditation with Flint

To begin with, sit comfortably and close your eyes. Place your stone in your lap and gently massage your temples in a circular motion with the palm or heel of your hands. Feel the tension of the day melt away, and your crown and third eye chakras unfold, opening to the higher realms.

Now massage your lower back, your kidneys and your tailbone, the base of your spine if you can reach it. Feel your lower chakras unwind and the heat of the earth begin to rise up your legs, up your spine, kindling the kundilini fire within you as it travels all the way up to your crown chakra.

Now pick up your piece of flint, and hold it in your hands. Breathe deeply, and feel the energy of the stone expanding and riding the kundilini energy with you. Feel your energy expanding, fueled by earth, fire and water energies. Feel your aura grow energized, the colors deepening in value and hue.

Flint has a deep connection to the earth and to spirit, and can connect you with their wisdom and strength. Your stone is open and ready to communicate with you now. What would you like to know?

Feel the wisdom that flint has shared with you integrate into your aura and merge with your cells, creating a deep, soul-based knowledge and healing. Feel your cells open and receive the energy of flint, the wisdom of source, and encode this new energy into your DNA. Feel yourself expand and rise with the new influx of energy. You are a renewable source of energy!

Thank your stone for all it has shared with you. Breathe some of your newfound energy and fire back into the stone.

The circle is complete.

Return, renewed.

Fluorite

"We are here to bring you balance. In your ever changing world, during ever changing times, we will balance and harmonize the waters that flow through your body. The more your vibration rises, the more susceptible you are to the energies that surround you, the frequencies that are emitted by the technology of your present reality, by ley lines, by organisms. We keep your own frequency tuned. We keep it humming as it should, the molecules of your physical reality aligned with the harmonies emitted from source. We help your cells ring with the sounds of angels, with the love of god, of all that is."

Fluorite, or the mineral calcium fluoride has an overall dissolving and re-ordering effect, which can benefit the body in a number of ways. For respiratory infections, its energy encourages the repair of mucous membranes. For skin problems, minor wounds, and ulcers, fluorite is good for regenerating new skin cells. For arthritis, this crystal can help dissolve build-ups and improve joint movement. Wherever there is disorder, the properties of fluorite will work to create order. In crystal healing, this mineral is also specifically known to reducc pain. Lay a stonc on a problcm area, or move it across the body, always in motion towards the heart. A gem elixir can also be made to utilize the healing energy of this stone.

Fluorite is a particularly beneficial healing crystal for the mind. It helps to link new information with what is already known, encouraging useful connections between ideas for deeper understanding. Beneficial for students and scholars alike, wearing fluorite earrings or keeping a sphere in the area for study, improves concentration and imparts a sharp mind. It works to dispel a myopic viewpoint, preconceived notions, and illusions.

The metaphysical properties of fluorite make this crystal a wonderful tool for psychic healing and spiritual development. It acts to protect from outside influences, manipulation, and mental influence. It also has a purifying effect on the aura and chakras, removing negative energy. With its penchant for order, any stress, chaotic energy, or psychological disorder will be directed towards calm, clear structuring.

Fluorite is capable of speeding spiritual awakening. By releasing ingrained belief systems and clearing the mind, it encourages intuition and individual spiritual awareness. Its use in meditation and psychic healing builds a connection with the universal. This same energy brings solidarity to a group of people.

If you are one of those people that has a hard time being around others because they seem to drain you, then wearing a piece of fluorite will act as a shield and protect you from those energies.

Fluorite will also absorb the negative energies and EMF waves that computers or other electronics give off. By placing a fluorite stone near your computer you are allowing the stone to absorb those energies instead of you. Just be sure to clean, clear and recharge your stone often!

Fluorite should be cleansed often due to its remarkable ability to absorb negative energies. It should be cleaned at least once a week, and if used in healing or self-healing after each therapy session. It can be cleansed by using running water for several minutes.

Meditation with Fluorite

Breathe in. Breathe out. Feel your body. Just feel it, as it is. How do you feel? Are you happy? Are you whole? Are you tired? Are you energized? Feel your body, just as it is, and let your mind relax into your body. Just feel your self.

Relax. Be at peace. All is well here, you are well here. You can be and do anything you want to do. We are fluorite, and we wish to help you with this work. So, let's begin by relaxing the cells in your body to a point where they can flow with the energy and vibrancy that they were intended. Let us help your body rejuvenate itself to the way it was meant to be. Let us encourage your body to be healed, perfect and whole.

Hold us. Hold us in your hands and allow us to help you heal. Allow us to help you become your true self.

Just sit now, and be. Just sit now, and hold us. Hold us, as we hold on to you.

Keep us with you, keep us near you. We are so excited to work with you! Make sure you bathe us often, just as you bathe your selves. We feed on the flow of water, on the cleansing energies of water.

We are one with the flow of life. Let us bring the flow to you, into you.

Breathe in, and awaken to life!

When you are ready, return. Return to the room and open your eyes.

Fulgurite

"Boom! Flash! That's how we come in, that is how we fulgurites are born. We are the voice of the cloud people, the emotions of the sky elementals. We bring wisdom from the sky realms down to earth, raising the vibration of the continents through the powers of fire and air. Use us to ignite radical change in your life, to energize your body and open you up to new ideas and ways of being. We are not quiet. We are not still. We carry the pure active energy of the divine, the wrath of the angels and the might of the originals."

Fulgurite, also known as "The Finger of God", is a special form of quartz glass that is created when lightning strikes sand or quartz-rich soil. "Fulgur" is latin for lightning. The lightning melts the sand, often forming strangely shaped tubes and forks as it goes. Most fulgurites are found in the desert or on beaches, with the majority on the market coming from the Sahara, Gobi and American Southwest deserts.

Meditation with Fulgurite will connect you with your higher self and Source mind. Fulgurite can work with any chakra and can help people ground, but it is especially attuned for work with the crown chakra or for activating kundalini (body lightning) energy. Many people use fulgurite to empower their prayers or rituals, and believe it will empower any attempt at manifestation or using the law of attraction. Often, the tubes are used to gently breath one's vision into being, sending it directly to Source and into the Earth's living matrix to manifest on the physical plane. Placing a piece on each chakra, with two additional pieces below the feet and above the head (using 9 in all), will result in full activation of kundalini, as well as ignite a healing process throughout the entire body.

Fulgurite can also help your psychic abilities manifest, particularly clairaudience (clear hearing). If you are interested in channeling or receiving intuitive information to help heal others, fulgurite can help you with this. Part of fulgurite's magic is that it can help you (and others) clear away old, habitual patterns that are no longer beneficial.

Meditation with Fulgurite

Imagine your stone, and close your eyes. Breathe in, and breathe out. Feel the pulse of the earth flow through you as you breathe in, and out.

Ba boom. Ba boom. Ba boom.

Breathing in, and breathing out.

Ba Boom. Ba boom. Ba boom.

Imagine what you would like to accomplish this month. See your goal, strong in your mind. See it take shape. Imagine all the details of this goal as it is fulfilled. Do not worry about envisioning how it will come about, just focus on your final outcome.

See how your goal will uplift yourself and those around, see how its manifestation will be for the highest good of everyone involved. Intend that it is so. Now breathe on your stone, as you hold that vision clearly in your mind.

Feel the power of source flowing through you, and breathe onto the stone again, source energy blasting through you and activating your intention, pushing your visualization out into the world to manifest on the physical plane.

Relax, breathe in, and breathe out, and know that it will be so.

Take some time now to sit with your stone and ask it how it would like to work with you in the future.

All is well. Your vision is taking root out in the world, and becoming real, here and now, in the physical realm. All will be well.

Take a deep breath in, and a deep breath out, and return.

Fuchsite

"Fuchsite holds the essence of all-one-peace within its shining form. Fuchsite is a stone intricately connected to the overlighting angels and nature devas of your world, and as such it can connect you with the PEACE that is your divine birthright. Let fuchsite smooth the rough edges from your day, let fuchsite sooth your spirit and show you how to just be. To be in the moment, to be at one with all moments, all the time, always, never rushing, never worried, that is the gift of the fuchsite, the divine all-one state of being that will benefit humanity more than any other lesson ever could."

Fuchsite enhances the power of other minerals and is a great stone to use during healing sessions because it will increase energy transfer when multiple stones are used for healing. It enhances knowledge and "right action". Fuchsite enhances your connection the nature spirits/devas and love and appreciation of beauty in nature. It cleanses and protects the auric fields of everyone who is near it. Fuchsite helps us to understand issues concerning our daily lives; such as stress, physical health, routines, career and environment. Fuchsite teaches true self-worth, assisting in the elimination of a tendency towards martyrdom or issues of servitude. Fuchsite helps to overcome codependency and aids in a speedy recovery from trauma, both emotionally and physically. It shifts energy into positive channels, therefore releasing blockages caused by excess energy. Fuchsite stabilizes spinal column alignment and increases flexibility in the musculoskeletal system. It treats repetitive strain injury, carpal tunnel syndrome and also aids in balancing the red and white blood cell ratio.

Fuchsite is the green variety of muscovite, gaining its color due to the high concentrations of chromium. When fuchsite is contained within quartz, it is referred to as green aventurine. Physically, fuchsite is one of those great minerals for people who have challenges with balancing blood sugar levels, and hence experience fluctuating mood swings as a result. The use of fuchsite crystal essence is a great remedy for this situation. Simply take a few drops after each meal to decrease your severe highs and lows.

Meditation with Fuchsite

 Close your eyes and open your mind. Feel the stresses, the worries, the annoying moments of the day fade away and every happy moment, every smile, every laughter, every ray of sunshine be remembered. Feel your joy and happiness flowing through you, bubbling up from the souls of your feet to the top of your head. Feel the laughter and the smiles fill you up, lift up, heal you up.

Now feel your consciousness expanding. Throw the doors to your mind wide open, hold your feet firmly on the ground and open your heart, your soul, your arms spread wide and ready to both give and to receive. Love flows in, and love flows out.

Love flows in, and love flows out.

Love in.

Love out.

Your spirit stands tall and strong, filled with love and universal life energy. You are like the strong trees that stand outside, the willows and the pines, the poplars and birches, flowing the will of Source through you, healing and uplifting the entire world as you are peaceful and present here in the NOW.

This is the energy of the stone you hold. This is the message of fuchite. You are all. You can heal the world completely, all on your own. You hold all the power of source, for you ARE all the power and love and determination of Source. You can remake the world in your image. Be sure it is the image you are wanting to bear. Let us now sit in the slow of this energy and commune with our stones.

Gather up your energy. Gather up your love. Keep all the love and power of source with you. It is your birthright. Never give it up.

This meditation is complete, just as you are whole, loved and perfect.

Golden Apatite

"We rise above. We rise above pain, we rise above greed, we rise above difficulty. We rise above earthly drama and trauma. We rise above, into the gracious energy of upliftment, of source. We hold the keys to the kingdom of source, and we can take you there with us. We take you out of the mundane, out of the little worries and stresses, and show you what really matters, so you can get out of your own way and into the where you really want to be."

Apatite is a high phosphate mineral that can be found in many colors including green, yellow, blue, brown and clear. Its name derives from the Greek word for "deceiver" because it was so often mistaken for other minerals such as aquamarine, tourmaline and peridot. "Yellow, or Golden, Apatite is found most readily throughout the Americas, as well as Norway and Russia. Golden apatite can range from a warm yellow to a greenish yellow, but should not be confused with green apatite, which is much darker and greener and carries a very different energy.

Golden apatite increases self-confidence and self-worth. It works with the solar plexus to return you to a more natural state of joy and security, helping release stress and fear. It can be used to enhance creativity, learning and focus, and is a wonderful stone for indigo children to work with.

It creates a willingness to let go of useless aspects of life, people and objects so that one can more easily manifest what is really needed and wanted in one's life. Try combining it with citrine to help manifest more financial abundance in your life.

Physically, it acts as a hunger suppressant and helps the body shed excess weight through the elimination of toxic anger and emotions stored in fatty tissues. Simply wear or carry a piece with you throughout the dayIt balances the physical, emotional, mental and spiritual bodies as well as the chakras. It has an uplifting effect on the nervous system, helping alleviate chronic fatigue and depression.

Fun Fact: Apatite is the mineral that makes up the teeth in all vertebrate animals as well as their bones.

Meditation with Golden Apatite

Breathe in the air. Breathe it in. Let it fill you up, flow through you, and remove the toxins from your body that you have accumulated throughout today. Breathe in the air, and release the stress. Release the worry. Release the doubt. Breathe in the air, and feel your self filling up with warmth, with the radiance of source. You are good. You are filled with good. You are good.

Feel your body taking in the yellow light of the sun, filling up with Source radiance, filling up with joy and sweetness, happiness and excitement. Feel every cell in your body lighting up with the yellow rays of healing light. Feel old hidden emotions bursting out of your cells as they are filled with the yellow rays, lighting up dark corners of your body and your soul, filling you up with radiance as the darkness streams out of your body.

Your body releases the old toxins easily, with no fear or sadness. You are filled with joy. You are filled with light. You feel good.

Now take a moment to sit with apatite, because it has a message for you. It has come to you today to remove your old fears and toxic emotions, and replace them with light and radiance. How can you best work together to achieve that goal? Apatite knows. Take some time now together.

Now breathe in, and breathe out. Thank your stone for its wisdom and healing. Gather your light together, sealed within your aura like a shield of divine fire, and bring yourself fully back into your body, back into your chair. Take a deep breath in, and a deep breath out. And return.

Green Aventurine Pyramid

"We are power. We are energy. When we were young, we held the spark of love and healing in us. Then we were shaped. Then we were hewn. Now we are fully realized, and our spark has become a flame that we use to help others become fully realized. Our love has become greater, more concentrated, a beam of healing energy that we send out into the universe in a constant pulsing stream. Heal, we say. Love, we say. Grow, we say. Our energies are strong. We are strong. Become, we say. Realize who you are, we say."

Aventurine is a form of quartz that contains plate-like inclusions, giving it a glittering effect known as "aventurescence." Green aventurine generally contains fuchsite. While green is most common, aventurine comes in a variety of other colors, including peach, orange, yellow, red, brown, purple, blue, and gray. The name derives from the Italian for "by chance" and it is considered a lucky stone of prosperity and abundance.

Green Aventurine is a joyful stone that helps calm the heart and solar plexus chakras, stimulating love and forgiveness, and a natural release of fear. Working with aventurine can help dissolve old blockages, fear-based beliefs and patterns of behavior. This naturally creates the space in one's life to attract people and opportunities that are more in alignment with your soul path. Life becomes easier with green aventurine around.

Physically, green aventurine has long been used to stimulate overall healing, and benefit the heart and liver specifically. Used topically as a crystal elixir spray, it is reported to help with skin issues such as rosacea and eczema. Many people also use it for guarding against the effects of pollution, EMF waves, radiation, and chemtrails. Judy Hall recommends taping a small piece to your cell phone or Bluetooth.

Pyramid shaped stones, like naturally-occurring apophyllite or carved pyramids, raise and concentrate energy. When held, they help open the crown chakra to the heavens. When placed under things (or people) they will direct that energy into the object. Many people like to charge their drinking water over crystal pyramids. Only a few minutes of charging is necessary, and more than 10 minute can actually result in one feeling over-stimulated or drained.

Meditation with
Green Aventurine Pyramid

Begin this meditation with four deep breaths.

Each breath stabilizes you, connects you to the earth, grounds you.

You are strong. You are relaxed.

Imagine your stone in both hands and breathe deeply. Know that you are connected with all of creation in this moment. You can feel everything around you, the air, the water, the earth, the sun. Think about what it is you would like to let go of, what no longer serves you, and exhale it out of your body. Feel all of it leaving your body, leaving your reality. The issue is a non-issue. You are perfect in every way.

Now think about who you are. What you are about. What you value. And now think about who your soul is. What your soul is about. What your soul values.

See the light of source flowing into your pyramid and filling it with the truth of who you really are. Breathe in, and the light of source flows up your arms, through your body, shifting you. You arc your soul, and your soul is you. Feel the shift in your vibration as the light of source fills you, as you soul fills you with true knowing. Take some time now to commune with your self, and with your stone.

You are whole. You are blessed. And you are ready. Return.

Grossular Garnet

"We are awake! Unlike our brown and red cousins, we embody the living energies of the earth, the flowers and the grasses, and most of all the trees. Our cousins strengthen the body, we enliven it. We wake you up on a cellular level. We are like chlorophyll for the soul. Try us, and you will see. We bring instant growth, instant energy, instant newness."

Grossular Garnet (aka Gooseberry Garnet) is a calcium aluminum silicate. It is most commonly found in shades of yellow and green, although it may also be brown or red. It is found primarily in Siberia, Brazil, California, Kenya and Tanzania.

Green grossular is believed to help balance the emotions with logic and benefits the heart chakra and related organs (lungs, heart, bone marrow, liver). Having a hard time connecting on a personal level? Is stress ruining your relationships at home? Try using grossular to lighten the mood and enhance heart-centered connections and communication. Many people find it to be very helpful at settling arguments for the highest good of all involved, and it may be useful during litigation.

Greet garnet carries the lively energy of growth and renewal, and it is believed to increase fertility and abundance both on all levels. Meditate with it for manifestation and creative visualizations, then watch the prosperity flow in!

Grossular is believed to have strong Angelic connections and may be used to connect with the higher realms or to draw their presence into your life for blessing.

Meditation with Grossular Garnet

Breathe deeply. Relax your mind, your body, your soul. Imagine that you are inside a warm, comfortable home, surrounded by light and love. You are happy and full of easy thoughts. You are relaxed, and fulfilled.

This home may be your current home, or the home you are currently creating on the manifestational etheric plane right now, the home that is waiting for you patiently until the time is right for you to move in.

See the life you live in this home. Feel how happy you are at the end of the day. Your needs are met, your family is comfortable, and all is well. See what that means for you. See how it looks. Feel it. Pull that feeling around you like a warm cloak.

Grossular Garnet is here with you tonight, helping you create the life you want. It is ready to co-create with you to manifest the life you are meant to live. Are you ready? Sit with your stone now in your perfect home, in your happy, fulfilled, comfortable life, and spend some time harmonizing together to make that life a fully realized reality.

All is well.

Look around your home, and set your garnet in a place of importance in the room, perhaps on a table, or an altar or a mantel. Know that your garnet will continue to work with you from this etheric realm to help you manifest the reality you are meant for.

Thank your stone, send feelings of love to your home, and return here, to this room, into your body, all the way in down to your toes.

All is well.

You are blessed.

Hematite

"Shield yourself. This is the message you receive all the time from your ego. You are always thinking about how to protect yourselves from other people, from disaster, from your fears. We show you there is nothing to fear. It is not that we are protective, as so many of you say, but that we remove the fear and the perceived need for self-preservation which so many of you feel at so many moments during your lives. We return you to the simple state of just being and acting, how you were as a child before you were taught the rules and told "don't do this", "don't do that," "now's not the time." It's always the time. It is always right. You have NOTHING to fear. Truly. You can do and be whatever you want. So smile. Show your appreciation and your happiness to everyone around you. Smile at your enemies. Smile at your friends. Smile at the sun, moon and stars. Smile, and be radiant, and be delighted and delight-full. We are a mirror of truth, we reflect your soul-smile, your true face, back to you so that you can really live."

Hematite is a form of iron oxide that is harder than pure iron. It's name comes from the greek word for blood, as its unpolished form can oxidize to a deep blood red. It tends to be most frequently associated with the base chakra, although I feel that it is highly attuned with the silver rays of the crown chakra. Many find it to be quite grounding and protective, due to its tendency to help us feel safe and increase our life energies. It is known as a stone for the mind, often being used to enhance memory and concentration.

As a slightly magnetized stone, hematite helps to align the polarities in our bodies, connecting our meridians and augmenting our own geo-magnetic alignments. It helps to balance our body, mind and spirit, connecting all our chakras from the base up through our crown chakra to our higher selves.

It is a very strong, energized stone, and some people can find it a bit difficult to work with. If you have a hard time letting go, hematite might be a bit of a challenge for you since it overrides the fears of the ego with the delights and confidence of the soul. It is often characterized as a very yang, male stone, but actually I feel that hematite is simply source. Neither male nor female, simply power without sex or predisposition.

Physically, hematite helps restore circulation and increase red blood cell production. It is beneficial for structural, physical issues of all kinds, from scarring to tears to wounds and breaks.

Cleanse hematite regularly by the light of the sun or moon. Avoid washing or directly infusing hematite in water due to its high iron content and potential for oxidation.

Meditation with Hematite

Gather closely and imagine your hematite stone in front of you. Close your eyes and imagine yourself in your favorite healing place. Open your heart. Open your mind. You are safe here. You are free.

We want you to see yourself in your healing space holding your stone in your hands. Begin to rub your stone between your hands like a piece of soap, now rubbing your stone over your arms, your torso, your face, up and down your legs. Feel the coolness of your stone imbuing your body and your being with strength and power. Feel the surety of your mind. You are a god in your body. You are divine. Continue washing your body, and see your aura developing a silver glow, glistening and gleaming around you as a pure, divine source of energy. See the silver light glittering and glowing around you, above you. See the light of source streaming into your crown chakra, feeding and growing your silver aura.

You are pure.

You are perfect.

Now settle down and feel the power through you, connecting you to your neighbor, your friends. Feel your self as you really are. Whole. Connected. Empowered. A Creator.

Let the messages of hematite come to you now, flowing to you and through you. Listen to your stone. Each is different, and yet each is the same. A part of the whole, embodying all that is at once, now and forever.

This is your time. This is your year, your hour, your minute. You are here, now, and the world is here for you. Return now to this room, to your here and now and remember what you have felt. Remember what you have learned.

Return.

Hemimorphite

"We have been waiting. We have been watching. We are clear. We are bright. We harness the light and the energy and we shine it all around us. We show you the way through the darkest night, through the brightest light. We illuminate the shadows and show you the way. We are pure. We are bright."

Hemimorphite is a hydrous zinc silicate found in Mexico, Africa, Italy, Greece, Germany, Thailand, and the United States. It is most frequently as a smooth blue or violet druzy crust, although it also (more rarely) forms in clear crystalline fan-shaped clusters. It is almost always found with smithsonite, another high vibration stone formed from zinc carbonate.

Hemimorphite activates the chakras in the body and opens your higher chakras to the light of source. It wants to help us reach our full potential. Calming and relaxing, it opens the body to the spirit of forgiveness and peace. It allows us to remain in balance and appreciate all our emotions as creative expressions of life energy. Hemimorphite is believed to be activated by touch, instantly attuning to the bearer and becoming stronger the more it is used.

It is considered a very high vibration stone with strong protection and healing abilities. It helps us disconnect from our earth-bound ego, dissolve negative emotional patterns and gain greater confidence. Use it to combat insecurity issues, sadness or depression. It is a wonderful stone for those searching for inner peace.

Blue hemimorphite is especially calming and opens up new avenues of communication. It is helpful to those who would work as psychic channels.

Physically, hemimorphite is used by crystal healers to balance hormones and heal dis-ease in the chest and head. It is also said to help bring out our inner beauty and relieve pain.

Meditation with Hemimorphite

To begin, sit comfortably and imagine your stone in your hands, taking three deep breaths.

Breathe in, and breathe out. Relax your muscles. Breathe in and out. In and out.

Calm your mind, release your thoughts.

Allow your entire being to relax. Easy. Easy. Calm.

Feel your consciousness sinking, safe and slow, as you go deeper and deeper into the darkness of your inner mind, as you reach your inner point of stillness.

Here in the center of your being, deep in your mind's eye, see yourself quiet, at peace, and whole. See yourself stand up, and walk through the darkness into a cool cave deep in the earth.

You feel safe here, secure, and very protected.

You run your hand along the walls of the cavern and can feel the vast wisdom of the ages surrounding you.

In the middle of the cave, you see the great mother of the hemimorphite stone you are holding, the piece from which your own was birthed, and you approach it with reverence.

It welcomes you to the cavern, and asks you to sit and speak with it.

146

You show the mother stone the small piece of hemimorphite in your hand, and ask her to bless it. Now, ask the stones if there is a particular name your piece would like to be addressed by, and introduce yourself. Explain what your intentions are, and what you are currently desiring in your life or needing help.

Ask the stones what way would be best for you to work with your piece, and if it has any particular messages for you.

Thank the mother and your stone for their blessings and their help. Stand up, and walk back the way you came. See yourself deep in the darkness, deep in your body, once again.

Breathe deeply. In. And out.

In and out. Relax.

Return.

Herkimer Diamond

"We shine into the night and lead the way into a new era. For those who want to explore and expand the universe, we have always lead the way. We helped the first peoples find their way to earth. We literally navigated the universe for them. Tap into our powers and navigate the flow of your planet, learn how to conserve your energy and expand your abilities in ways you have never imagined. We hold all the knowledge. We can take you there."

Herkimer Diamonds are double terminated quartz crystals with 18 facets (six sides and two terminations), named after their place of first discovery in Herkimer, NY. They can be extremely clear, cloudy, or a dark smoky color. Common inclusions include enhydros (with fluid such as water, oil or methane bubbles inside) or black, yellow, and brown hydrocarbons and anthraxolite. Marcasite, dolomite, and pyrite can also be found in herkimers. Since their initial discovery in Herkimer, they have been found in Arkansas and the Himalayas of Tibet and China.

Herkimers hold amplified quartz energy and are considered an ascension stone. They will significantly boost the energy of other stones through their electromagnetic pulses. These pulses also affect our bodies' electromagnetic field, and is believed to boost clairaudience, telepathy, and other psychic gifts. Herkimers connect us to higher realms and angels, and enhydros are used in particular to help resolve and release emotional issues.

Many people use herkimers to clear the chakras and improve energy flow in and around the body. They are believed to help alleviate geopathic stress, radioactivity and EMF effects, and were been used for centuries by Native Americans in the Northeast before European colonization as protective healing talismans. Because of its strong clearing abilities, many people use it to help ease addictive behaviors and eliminate toxins from the body.

Meditation with Herkimer Diamond

Hold your stone and breathe deeply.

Breathe in, and breathe out.

Breathe in, and breathe out.

Relax. As you breathe in, imagine the cells in your body awakening. Feel your cells energizing, opening. As you breathe in and out, your body feels lighter and lighter, more and more radiant. You are filled with light. You are filled with energy. Your stone pulses with light, triggering your cells to gleam. Your DNA lights up throughout your body, fully activated and awakened. Damaged cells begin to repair themselves, older cells begin to reverse their deterioration, reversing aging processes. Corrupted DNA sequences are replaced with an original divine blueprint.

Your feel more alive, more awake.

You are.

You are wide awake. Your senses are heightened. You DNA is fully turned on and your tapped in to all your natural abilities and the creative potential of Source. You are limitless. Revel in this feeling for now.

Now, pull yourself back in a little, bring in some of that energy and focus it on your stone. Herkimer has a message for you. Spend some time now listening to your stone – what has it come to teach you? How can you work together for your highest good?

Now, pull yourself in a little more. Keep your DNA turned on and tapped in, but bring your focus back in to your consciousness, back into your body. Thank your stone for the time it has spent with you and the for the great healing it has facilitated, and return fully back into your body. Back into your radiant, pure activated body.

All is well. You are limitless.

Return.

Indicolite

"Indicolite connects you to the mysteries of your soul. It is helpful for all inner and outer seeking, for adventures within and without. Indicolite with quartz allows you to see and hear its messages even more clearly, with the quartz acting a sort of intermediary or interpreter between our human physical minds and the extremely high source vibration of the indigo ray. This stone will clear out your oldest, deepest and darkest patterns, and help lift you into the higher realms. This is a good place to start, a good place to begin your transformation into the best and the brightest stars that you already are."

Indicolite is the rarest color of tourmaline, its current name deriving from the older name of "indigolite" referring to the desirable dark blue color. Tourmaline increases flexibility, happiness, objectivity, compassion and serenity. It also enhances tolerance and understanding. It is a stone that is very helpful for channeling. Tourmaline is also a very protecting stone. Indicolite has the same healing properties as all other tourmalines, but the gemstone's magnesium and iron adds a surplus. It improves the metabolism in general and reduces decalcification of the skeletal system.

It corresponds to all chakras in terms of clearing, but particularly to the throat and third eye chakras. It is said to aid in the quest for spiritual growth. It increases psychic awareness, and increases healing powers. Indicolite can also bring happiness and laughter to your life. It also promotes inspiration of all kinds, and lessens fear. Indicolite is a protective stone that can dispel curses and protect from all dangers.

Indicolite gives rest during meditations. Its intense blue color radiates harmony, it makes people both honest and tolerant and it is the best pain killer in the whole spectrum of colors. Indicolite has a direct and healing influence on the nervous system, so you can insure yourself of a good night's rest by laying the stone under your pillow.

Indicolite has a relaxing effect, stimulates creativity, love, faithfulness, devotion, patience and offers mental protection. It's an ideal meditation stone and an excellent aid in the quest for spiritual growth.

It facilitates communication and psychic awareness, it's a wonderful stone for aligning with the higher self for deep insight, vision, intuition. It also promotes self – healing. Indicolite may stimulate a life of prayer, solitude and meditation, encouraging you to find your own spiritual path, to aim for spiritual freedom.

Indicolite also helps in case of constipation and infertility. It supports the immune system and protects all physical functions.

Meditation with Indicolite

Breathe in. Breathe out.

Release the day. Let your mind wander.

Breathe in source energy.

Breathe out the debris you picked up since the last time you were here.

Relax.

Feel yourself sinking deep into your seat, relaxing, letting go. Let it all go. Be at peace.

What are you holding on to that is not yours to work through?

What are energy patterns are weighing you down?

See the color surrounding shift from mere darkness to the deepest, richest blue. See rays of indigo light surround you, emanating from your own third eye and swirling around you, growing and illuminating the darkness around you in a serene, living light. Hear the voice of your own indicolite crystal, giving you advice and instructions for how it would like to be included in your life over the coming month. Does it have a name or an energy that it would like you to be aware of? Sit now bathing in the blue radiance with your crystal.

It is time for the radiance to recede, gathered into your third eye and returned to your body and soul. Bundle up all the lessons and energies you have acquired here tonight and store them inside of you. Breathe in the energy.

You are ready.

Return.

Kyanite

"Black. Green. Blue. Orange. White. Gray. We all work the same. We all align the waters in your body so that your energies can flow properly. We allow the meridians to connect, the chakras to flow, and your mind and body to be fully open and receptive to the intentions of your true self, your own source energy. We facilitate balance and flow. Nothing more. Nothing less. When you are balanced, you are able to manifest all that you want and need, and see your path most clearly. When you are flowing, you are joyful and easy, and the world flows with you."

The name "Kyanite" derives from the greek word for deep blue, kyanos. It is a silicate mineral characterized by a diamond-like cleavage in one direction and two separate hardnesses, making it a challenging stone to cut or facet. Kyanite clears and aligns the chakras of all those who come near it. When it is worn, it has a constant protective and grounding effect as it clears and aligns the chakras, clears and aligns the energy systems of the body, over and over again. The bearer of this stone is quite difficult to knock off-balance energetically. Because the chakras are aligned and open, one's higher self and energy body are able to enter the physical body, leading to higher ascension and attunements. Qi and kundalini energies flow better throughout the entire body when kyanite is around. Because it enhances energy flow and calms the central nervous system, it promotes feelings of tranquility and peace.

Kyanite is easily found in many shades of blue and green, as well as orange and black: black Kyanite is considered more protective but less aligning than blue Kyanite, while the green focuses its healing energy more on the physical body. Regardless of its color, Kyanite is able to attune the wearer to his or her true path, opening channels of creativity, dreaming and visualization.

Physically, Kyanite can assist in pain management and glandular disorders. It is also believed to be effective against fevers and infections because it helps return the body to its natural state of perfection.

Meditation with Kyanite

Imagine your stone in your hands and relax.

Allow yourself to come into alignment.

Feel the energy of source flowing into your crown chakra, down through your third eye, down your spinal column, through your throat chakra, down into your heart, through your solar plexus, into your diaphragm and your abdomen, down through your pelvis, to your knees, to your feet, and back up again.

Feel the energy flowing through you, around you, circulating and energizing your body and mind.

Feel your worries leaving your body, and the love and assurance of source, of God, of your true self flowing through you.

Feel how perfect you are.

Feel how connected you are.

Be at peace.

Be easy.

Communicate now with your stone and your higher self. Allow yourself to dialogue with each of them, with all of you and all of source.

Now thank your stone and your higher self for their guidance and loving energies.

Take time to appreciate this enhanced feeling of energy in your body. This is how you are supposed to feel all the time. Revel in it. Get used to it. Claim it.

You are whole.

You are blessed.

You are complete.

Return.

Lapis Lazuli

"Lapis Lazuli was the stone of the gods. It was used to access immense amounts of electrical power by the ancients, and later shamans used it successfully to create an open dialogue with the powers that be. Use Lapis to tap into ALL that IS. Use Lapis to bring new levels of wealth and harmony into your life. Lapis can align you to your Divine Blueprint, with your True Path, the Path with a Heart, the life you are wanting and meant to be living. Many of you are close, so close already. This stone will bring you closer."

The main component of lapis lazuli is lazurite (25% to 40%), a feldspathoid silicate mineral. Lapis itself is considered a rock, not a mineral – minerals conatin only one component, while lapis lazuli also contains calcite (white), sodalite (blue), and pyrite (metallic yellow).

Lapis has been highly valued for many thousands of years. The most famous locality for fine quality lapis lazuli is in the same ancient deposit high in the mountains of Afghanistan where it was originally mined at least 6000 years ago. It was said to impart ancient knowledge, and the wisdom to use it and to enhance one's awareness, insight and intellect.

Ground lapis was the secret of the blue in ultramarine, the pigment which painters used to paint the sea and the sky until the nineteenth century. The ancient city of Ur has had a thriving trade in lapis as early as the fourth millennium B.C. The name is international, from the Latin, lapis, which means stone, and from the Arabic, aula, which means blue.

All cultures have used lapis to decorate the statures of the deities. It has always been greatly valued by rulers, being used for both magical and medicinal purposes.

A stone of protection that may be worn to guard against psychic attacks, Lapis Lazuli quickly releases stress, bringing deep peace. It brings harmony and deep inner self-knowledge. Encourages self-awareness, allows self-expression and reveals inner truth, providing qualities of honesty, compassion and morality to the personality. Stimulates objectivity, clarity and encourages creativity.

Lapis Lazuli boosts the immune system, purifies blood, lowers blood pressure, cooling and soothing areas of inflammation. It alleviates insomnia and vertigo, and overcomes depression. Lapis Lazuli benefits the respiratory and nervous systems and the throat, vocal chords, and thyroid, cleanses organs, bone marrow and thymus. Lapis Lazuli helps female reproductive issues and PMS. Lapis Lazuli stimulates the thymus gland. Lapis Lazuli helps with insomnia, and migrane headaches.

Lapis Lazuli reminds us of the power of the spoken word and is one of the best stones to use when opening and balancing the Throat Chakra. Lapis encourages clear, full expression when sharing information with others, including an easier voicing/communication of anger.

A Third Eye Chakra opener, Lapis Lazuli connects the physical and celestial kingdoms. Deeply peaceful, Lapis provides wisdom into mystical realms and connection with spiritual guardians.

Lapis can be a key to spiritual attainment. Lapis is a good stone to expand intuitive skills while remaining objective and open to reasoned analysis. Lapis also protects against psychic attack, shielding negative energy and returning any negative vibrations to their source. Lapis Lazuli will enhance dream and spiritual work.

Meditation with Lapis Lazuli

Today is the beginning of the rest of your life. Close your eyes and embrace the darkness of the night. Embrace the feeling of the unknown. Your life spreads out before you with wonderful certainty. A certainty of love, fulfillment and removal of boundaries. Everything you came to do in this world is at your fingertips. You have done so much, and yet you have only just begun. Now is the time to let go of old patterns and fears. Your higher mind is calling to you. Spirit is calling you. We, the divine, are calling you.

Relax your mind, relax your heart and soul. Feel at one with the flow of the universe. Breathe us in. Breathe us out. Spirit in. Spirit out. Life. Love. Happiness.

Hold your Lapis up to your breastplate at your thymus, thyroid, or heart. You decide. You choose. This is your life. You do as you please. Allow the energy of Lapis to mingle with your aura, to filter through your energy body, and then your physical body. Feel the cool, calm, clear energy powering you up. Feel it flowing through you, washing away your uncertainty and doubt.

Spirit is hear for you. Your guides are here for you. The gods are here for you. Open your mind and receive their messages. See the life you are living for what it is: a journey for play and exploration, a time for growth and expansion. What's next? Sit now, and let us show you the way.

You are whole. You are here, you are complete. There is nothing to deny, nothing to retreat from. Embrace life, and live as you are wanting.

We are complete. Return.

Larimar

"Larimar brings you both the calm and power of the sea. The calm: the knowing that every tide out brings a tide in, the interconnectedness of all that dwell in the water, the cellular healing ability of the salted mineral waters. The power: the great waves that can wash away an island, the ability to mold rock and dissolve metal, the creative essence of the earth and all her fury. Larimar can help you make peace in the middle of a storm. It holds the knowledge of the earth's oldest history, the origin of your species, the story of all who have come before. It is the womb of your mother, the essence of your father. It is a stone of deep answers, and soothing wisdom."

Larimar is an extremely rare form of pectolite that has only been found in one location: a mountainous, relatively inaccessible region of the Dominican Republic overlooking the Caribbean Sea. This gemstone first surfaced in 1974, although the inhabitants of the region and their ancestors have long been aware of the stone. Legend has it that they used to simply collect these stones on the beach, but one day they couldn't find anymore. They went to explore upstream, and came upon a rock formation that seemed to be the source of this blue precious stone. The name Larimar was given to the stone by a Dominican, Miguel Méndez, who combined his daughter's name LARIssa, with MAR, the Spanish word for sea. The stone is also called the Atlantis Stone.

Larimar is finely tuned to the human body, especially the 5th chakra in the throat area of the body. Larimar benefits communication, supports the healing process (thymus), and increases the possibility of regulating thyroid gland malfunction.

Larimar supports dissolving different kinds of energy blockages that cause physical problems or mental diseases. It enables the flow of energy within a person and helps promote an open mind to changes and improvement. It also softens the stress and tension that problems bring.

It is no coincidence that Larimar has appeared at a time when the world is going through important transformations. The blue gemstone softens, enlightens and supports the healing process of the physical, emotional-mental and spiritual bodies.

It combines our mind and thoughts (elements of air energy) with our heart and emotions (elements of water energy), gathering them into a harmonious whole. In addition, Larimar helps us to view events from a different, more positive perspective.

Meditation with Larimar

Close your eyes, and relax. Let the stresses of the day ease away from your body. Breathe them out. Allow the pure, clear air in, cleansing your soul, and breathe out all your tension, all your worries, all your sorrows.

Breathe in. Breathe out.

Let in the clearing. Breathe out the day.

Let in the healing. Breathe out the day.

Relax. Be easy. Be calm.

Imagine yourself on a quiet stretch of sandy beach, no people, just the birds flying here and there and the soothing crashing of the waves nearby. The waves come in, the waves go out. The gulls swoop down, catch fish, and fly away. Hermit crabs skitter to and fro on the sand, the sun peeks out from fluffy white clouds above, and is hidden again while a refreshing breeze caresses the palm trees.

You rest.

And then you rise. You walk along the beach, letting the waves kiss your feet, looking for shells. You see a small twinkle of blue sky in the sand, bend down and find a smooth, soft stone, the color of the sea and the sky. You hold it, and feel overwhelmed with a sense of peace. There is nothing to do for it, except sit, hold the stone and relax.

You sink down into the sand, and stare out at the sea. A voice fills your ears, and the stone speaks to you. Listen to its message.

Ask the stone if there is any special way it would like you to work with it, and if it has a particular name or use. Sit with the stone.

Now rise up, walk back along the beach, and into this room, into your chair, and return your consciousness to your body.

Breathe in. Breathe out.

Wiggle your toes. Breathe in.

Return.

Larvikite

"We see your inner fire and answer with a flash and flare of our own. We teach you to let go of fear and shine. Dazzle the world. Do what you will. There is only here, and now, what are you waiting for? We hold the beauty and the light of creation within us, we harness the energy of the Great Central Sun and the Aurora Borealis, and mirror it back to you, always to you, so that you may shine, shine, shine."

Larvikite is a relative of Labradorite, another member of the feldspar family. Sometimes called black labradorite or black moonstone, it is a kind of granite found near the Larvik Fjord in Norway.

Larvikite benefits both the third eye and the root chakra. It is grounding and protective. It shields the wearer from negative energy and helps make one feel more comfortable amidst the most difficult situations. It is believed to be especially helpful for students and anyone learning to do something new or different, because it helps the mind cope and adjust while the brain is creating new pathways of information while increasing trust and confidence in our own thought processes. A calming stone, it is good for learning and concentration disorders. Larvikite can benefit meditative exercises, especially visualization and Akashic work.

Larvikite is wonderful for connecting with Earth energies is general, and the fairies in particular. It unleashes a joyful energy that allows us to connect more fully with the physical realm while enjoying our full, creative potential.

Physically, larvikite relaxes the nervous system; benefits skin, tissues and brain function; and may improve memory and blood pressure.

Meditation with Larvikite

Close your eyes and relax.

Breathe in deeply, hold for four counts, and breathe out.

Breathe in, hold, and breathe out.

Breathe in, hold, and breathe out.

Relax.

Breathe in. Breathe out.

Let go.

Imagine yourself outside on a clear, starry night. Comfortable, relaxed, you look up, and see the aurora borealis twirling and swirling above you. The lights dance all around you, a gentle breeze stirs your hair, kisses your skin, as you spin and dance with the lights that surround you. You become one with the aurora, and the Great Spirit moves you, in you, through you. You hold your stone, your larvikite, and you understand. You can hear Spirit, you can hear your higher self, your soul, and you know what you need, what you want. You know who and what you are. You know what to do.

Take some time now to commune with your true self, with larvikite by your side as your guide. What can you all accomplish together?

Take a deep breath. The stars are beginning to fade. Dawn is coming. The aurora borealis quiets down, the sky gets lighter and lighter. You feel calm. You feel whole. You feel ready to face the world, to face the day, to become a new tomorrow.

Take a deep breath, and return. Come back into this room, into your body, into your seat, grounded and connected from your crown down to the tips of your toes.

All is well.

Return.

Lepidolite

"Lepidolite flows directly with Source. See those sparkles? That is a physical representation of source. Wherever there is sparkle, you are invoking source love, source light, source creation. Lepidolote helps you tap in directly to the angels, god and the ascended masters. It connects you to all that is divine, all that is true, all that is you. It balances your chakras and enacts your ability to walk as a god upon the earth. Claim your birthright. Be divine."

Also known as "Peace stone" and "Lilalite" (Playful Stone), lepidolite is a form of mica discovered in the 1700s in the Czech Republic. The purple and pink mineral is also found in Brazil, Africa and the United States. Its color derives from lithium, which is no surprise when one considers the calming effect of this stone.

Lepidolite clears away negative energies and raises your vibration. It helps soothe the mind and body by connecting you with Source energy and Source love. Many people find it helpful to use during meditation and astral travel, because it is so adept at connecting us to our higher self. It can also be used to access the Akashic records or facilitate channeling. Use it to clear obstacles and create a new life.

Lepidolite combines well with rose quartz to help heal relationships, and is very nice used at night to create a restful atmosphere and induce deep sleep. It is deeply harmonizing and balancing. Use it to ameliorate grief and the emotional effects of trauma or abuse.

Physically, it is believed to help detoxify the body and heal DNA. It may be used to clear electromagnetic disturbances and calm the energy in a room. Because of its soothing effect, it is often recommended in cases of psychiatric imbalance or nerve disorders. It is also said to strengthen the immune system and help with allergies.

Meditation with Lepidolite

Let's close our eyes and relax. Take a few deep breaths, in and out, in and out.

In and out.

Relax.

As you breathe in, imagine the violet sparkles of lepidolite lifting up, riding the air around you. You are surrounded by purple sparkles, bathed in purple sparkles. Not dust, not powder, but pure, purple glimmering lights. The air you breathe is infused with this glimmer, and you begin to glow from within, a pure, sparkling being of light. You are radiant with the glow of source energy, filled with the light and the love of source. You feel love for all beings. You feel love for all times. You feel love for your self, and you feel love for your enemies.

You feel at peace. Your body is at one with your mind, at one with your higher self and you are filled with confidence that you know how to proceed in the coming months. You can feel, you know, that all will be well.

Now focus again on your stone. Ask if it has any special messages for you, any particular instructions. Does it have a name? Does it have something it wants you to know or to do? Spend some time now with your stone, and your inner sparkle.

175

Now it's almost time to return. Thank your stone for its messages, and see the sparkles in the air around you settling, consolidating around you and your stone. Draw this energy in, remember how it feels to sparkle and flow.

You are whole. You are well. You are radiant. Return now.

Limonite Pseudomorph After Pyrite

"We are small but we are full with power and purpose. We take the weight of the world and transmute it into new energy, lighter, joyful energy. What was once heavy and a difficult burden shifts to a higher level of being, bringing the world ever closer to the realms of light and love. Join us, lightworkers, and transform the world."

These little stones are cubes of pyrite that have decomposed, rusting and transforming into limonite. The limonite retains the shape of the original stone, those making it a pseudomorph (ps). Sometimes they have portions deep inside that are still pyrite, which gives them a greater weight.

Limonite is the form of hydrated oxidized iron. It can found as a lemony color varying to a deep chocolate brown, and is sometimes found included in or coating quartz – when it coats quartz the piece is referred to as a "golden healer" and is believed to carry highly amplified healing energies. Limonite itself is traditionally used to benefit skeletal and blood/liver issues in the body, as well as aid in general healing. Limonite can be used with great effect in distance healing sessions to facilitate emotional healing.

Limonite helps you acknowledge your higher purpose and follow your true path, the path with a heart. It improves the connection between the body and soul, transforming anger and old wounds into empathy and compassion. It heals scars and opens the heart chakra to the highest light and love emanations of mass consciousness, so that you can connect with other lightworkers and improve physical reality through the world.

Pyrite is also considered a very healing stone, bring activating kundalini fire energy in the body and balancing the masculine and feminine aspects of the self. When it transforms into limonite, a great healing has taken place, a merging of the yin and yang, representing the ascension of the self to a unified being, soul and body, spirit and physical vehicle, acting as one.

In sacred geometry, the cube is dubbed "Metatron's Cube" and is believed to contain all shapes ever created by God within it. The cube represents the flow of energy and creation of all patterns in the universe.

Meditation with
Limonite Pseudomorph Cubes

Hold your stone in your hand, and breathe deeply. Feel your body filling up with light with each breathe in, and your lungs expelling darkness with each breath out.

You breathe in the light. You exhale the dark. Breathe in light. Breathe out dark.

In your mind's eye, see yourself as a beacon of light. Stand, and you are as a pillar of light, radiant, glowing, pure. Look before you, and see another, larger beacon of light approaching. The pillar glows a brilliant pink and green, white and gold, and moves to stand in front of you.

This is the Archangel Metatron. He has been watching you for some time, recording your good deeds for all time in your Akashic records, and he would like to work with you this evening in a more conscious manner. He would like you to vow, tonight, to become one of his earth angels: one of those beings of light and positive energy who shifts the world around them towards ever-more positive levels. In return, he will help you clear old negative patterns from your light body, patterns you have accumulated from lifetime to lifetime, what you call karma, he is going to clear that for you now, tonight, for all time.

To begin with, he is going to install a metatronic cube within your breastplate. This cube is going to work for all time to insure that you do not accumulate more negative energy in the future, and help clear away etheric debris from your vicinity. You will be clear and full of light forever. This work is a great healing. Do not be in fear. If you wish it, Metatron will also place a secondary cube in your brow, to help you create light-thinking. This is a second gift. The third gift is the clearing that he is going to perform now on your soul and on your Akash. Your records are going to be cleared. This is a gift of more magnitude than you can begin to imagine. You are all great lightworkers, you who are reading this now. Metatron has been waiting for this day, for your line of healers to come to him. Let the healing begin.

*** Meditate for as long as you need. ***

You are now healed. You are well. You will not need to do this again for yourself, but every time you read or share this meditation, you will be spreading great light of source with the world, allowing the original patterning of the WORD to spread and heal mankind.

Go in light. Go in power. All is well.

Magnetite

"Have you forgotten what it feels like to fully connect with the earth and have all the energy of Source running through you? Have you forgotten what it was like to be a young child, with enough energy to fly but frustrated by your lack of wings and swift feet? We harness that energy for you, we can return you to that state. We will teach you what it means to really be in full alignment with your natural born capabilities and bring you back to that high energy state."

Magnetite, also known as Lodestone, is a kind of iron-rich spinel found in large deposits throughout the world that has natural magnetic properties. Its color can range from black to brown to red, and it may form as a rough ore, or in octahedrons. The octahedrons naturally connect us to pyramid energies and carry the highest vibration.

Magnetite is actually the most magnetic natural substance known to us on the planet and is believed to create much of the Earth's magnetic field, allowing birds and other animals to navigate. The human body actually creates and contains magnctitc, with high concentrations found in the spine and brain. Some scientists are studying the effects of magnetite on the brain and many believe that it may play a role in heightened sensory perception, including telepathy and dowsing.

Many people use Magnetite to attract beneficial energies into their life. Its highly magnetic, iron-rich nature aligns our physical blood with the purest vibrations of source and brings that which we need to us so that we can manifest our highest good. It is also a very grounding stone, bringing us into alignment with the planet so that we can manifest more easily on the earthly plane. It works very well to create a protective shield around people and spaces when worn or used in a grid, and can strengthen the entire aura.

Physically, it has often been used to balance the left and right hemispheres of the brain and the masculine and feminine poles of the body. This in turn can balance ones emotions, making it useful mood disorders stemming from chemical imbalances and hormone-related mood swings. It raises our energy in a positive way, so that if someone is anxious or over-stimulated, lodestone can actually have a sedative effect.

MORE ABOUT OCTAHEDRONS – The octahedron is the third platonic solid, a double pyramid sort of shape with eight sides that illustrates the concept of "as above, so below." It represents the Air Element and stones that exhibit this shape can help to balance the ego-mind with one's higher intellect, or soul. It is also used to balance and attune the heart chakra to higher capacities for nurturing and compassion.

Meditation with Magnetite

Hold one or more magnetite pieces in each of your hands. Close your eyes and breathe deeply, in and out. Relax, and breathe in. Relax, and breathe out. Feel your energy begin to shift and grow. You are a powerful being in powerful body. How could you have forgotten? You are strong. You are virile. You are alive. There is so much you can do.

Bring your hands up to your heart chakra and breathe in, feeling your energy continue to expand and connect to your soul, to the planet, to all that is.

Magnetite is here for you. It know what you came here to do. It knows what you are really capable of. If has been with you all this time, waiting for you to awake. The time is now. You are ready. Remember who you are, who you have come here to be, and what you are meant to do. Magnetite would like to help you, so spend some time now with your stones. What are you wishing to attract into your life? What are you wishing you could be or do? How would you like to positively shift your life here on earth? Magnetite can help you navigate the ways. Ask it how.

Now thank your stones, and let them know that you will help re-energize them in the sunlight over the next few days.

Thank them, and take a deep breath. It is time to return now, back into the room, back into your body. Breathing.

Mystic Merlinite™

"We are not connected to Merlin, but we are connected to Magic. The magic of the ages, the abilities of all beings to do more than they think they can. Use us to connect you to the untested capabilities coded and locked in your DNA. Dream big. We'll take you there."

Mystic Merlinite™ is Indigo Gabbro, a relatively newly discovered combination of quartz, feldspar and chlorite, serpentine, muscovite, pyroxene, hercynite, olivine and magnetite found in Madagascar and Alaska. It often contains valuable amounts of precious metals. It forms an integral part of the ocean floor, and as such may be used to connect us to both water and earth. Note: This stone is not the same as what many people call simply Merlinite, which is actually another name for Dendritic Opal or Druzy Psilomelene.

Mystic Merlinite™ helps us see both the light and the dark, the yin and the yang. It allows us to see what is hidden and repair it using the lighter aspects of spirit. It is so attuned to the lighter side, in fact, that it works as a beacon of light to attract beneficial guardian spirits, angels and guides. It is a great stone to use in prayer or ritual, because it helps attract the attention of higher realms. You can also use it to create a protective shield around you, as it naturally counteracts and transmutes negative energy coming in.

Mystic Merlinite™ also changed the energy you are harboring and sending out – any negative feelings of anger or self-loathing will be released and rebirthed as forgiveness and compassion. Use the stone to release old wounds and traumas on any level.

Physically, Mystic Merlinite™ may be used to help repair muscles and bruises, and to improve immune response.

Meditation with Mystic Merlinite™

Sit quietly and imagine a stone in your left hand.

Breathe deeply and hold the breath for four counts.

Exhale, and relax.

Breathe in, and feel your breath going deep into your diaphragm, into your solar plexus. Breathe out, and imagine all the worries of the day leaving your body.

Breathe in, and feel the warm air circulating energy and power throughout your entire body, through your legs and arms, your feet and your hands.

Breathe out, and relax.

See yourself by the ocean, warm and relaxed. Happy. You feel good. You feel whole.

Place your stone in your right hand, and walk into the ocean. Feel the sand in your toes. Feel the sun on your skin. You feel safe and secure. The ocean welcomes you, waves kiss your feet and your legs.

What is it you are wanting to do this month? Where are you wishing you could go, who do you want to be? Mystic Merlinite would like to help you on your quest. Wash your stone in the sea, wash your arms and your hands. Imagine the life you are wanting. There in the ocean, look at your stone, and open yourself to its energy. See what messages the stone might have for you. Allow the energy of Mystic Merlinite to infuse you, awaken you.

Your stone is going to work with you for the month and help you open to the magic of your true self. Breathe deeply, and know that this is so. Breathe out, and let your fears go.

Breathe in.

Breathe out.

In.

And Out.

And when you are ready, return to this world, to this room, to your body.

Return.

Meteorites from Sikhote Alin

"We come from a star system so far away that it has no name in your books. We hold deep knowledge from the creation of your solar system, because we were there when it began, when your planets were formed and your people began to be. We did not bring with us any seeds for life. We brought with us an effect of re-patterning, a reminder that life is not meant to be a struggle, that life on your planet was intended to be a beautiful, powerful thing. That all peoples were supposed to get along, that all peoples began together, with one plan. That all peoples wanted to create a world where the stars would work together for harmony, where darkness would have no place, where illness would never be, where all would have food, harmony, love and peace. This planet was meant to be the cradle of creation, a place where the Da Vincis of the Universe, the most innovative and creative, could be born. Unfortunately, darkness came soon to your planet, and corrupted the energies of the first peoples. We came, to hold the light in the world, to remind the fourth peoples of their mission, and to help the world cleanse itself of the dark. Use us for light. Meditate with us, and you will see the way, in all things, always."

At 10:38am on February 12th in 1947, a large meteor fell in the Sikhote Alin mountains in Southeastern Russia near Vladivostok, leaving an estimated 70-150 tonnes of debris over a half mile area. Composed primarily of iron (93.3%), the meteorite also contains nickel (5.3%), cobalt (0.5%), sulphur (0.5%), phosphorous (0.3%) and copper

(0.03%), as well as the minerals chromite, schreibersite and troilite.

Meteorites are generally considered to have an unusual, alien energy – who would have thought? Some people resonate strongly with meteorites and are very drawn to them, while others find their energy uncomfortable.

Many believe that meteorites can help us connect with extra-terrestrials and off-planet guides, and that they connect us to universal source energy. Other people believe that meteorites hold memories of ancient alien warfare and battles, and still others feel that meteorites have no energetic impact on earth bio-energy (ie: our bodies). Due to their high iron content, I find that meteorites can and do have a significant effect on our electromagnetic field, and can be used beneficially for meditation and healing, generally helping to increase the flow of Qi throughout the body and dissolving energetic blockages.

Long prized by astrologers and healers, meteorites are often carried as a protective talisman against fire and explosions. Some use it to overcome addictions and bad habits, and many find it helpful for dream and trance work.

Meditation with Sikhote Alin Meteorite

Hold your stone and breathe deeply.

Breathe in, and breathe out.

Breathe in, and breathe out.

Feel yourself here in this room, here on earth. Feel yourself on the planet, with the planet. Feel how you are connected to the energy here. Feel the spin of the planet, the orbit of the land around the sun, the tremors deep within the earth's core as it moves and shakes, shimmies and shifts. Feel how your energy responds to the planet, how when she aches, you ache, how when she shifts, you shift.

Now, bring your energy back in, and focus on the meteorite in your hand. How does your stone feel to you? Does it fit? Does it feel different? Can you distinguish between the aura of the meteor, and the energies of the earth? Let the magnetic pull of your skeleton draw in the iron energy of the meteorite in your hand, feel how your body responds, blockages dissolving away, energy patterns in your meridians shifting and changing, responding with a better flow and renewed vigor. Take some time now to relax with your stone, ask it any questions you want, find out how it would like to work with you in the coming weeks, if it has a name or a special message for you.

Now, thank your stone, and breathe in deeply. Feel yourself reconnecting with the earth. You are here, in the room, on the planet. You are whole, and you are well.

All is Well. Return.

Moqui Marbles

"We are pure power. We unleash the potential you hold locked and hidden away deep inside your human core. We work with your DNA to release your true potential. Many like to meditate with us because they feel it connects them to higher realms – this is not accurate. We connect you to your true selves, we release you from the prison of your DNA and allow you to begin a larger, greater life, an empowered existence. Shamans of old knew that to tap into us was to tap into true power and magic. Use us wisely, use us well."

Moqui Balls, also known as Shaman Stones, Thunderballs, Desert Marbles and Shamanic Star Stones, come from Navajo Sandstone and are scattered across miles of public and private land in Utah and Arizona. Concretions of sandstone coated with iron hematite, it used to be thought that they were formed when a meteor struck in the desert ranges, but in fact these marbles were created as water ran through the sandstone ranges. Two batches of stones can be found, one from around 25 million years ago, and another between 2 and 3 million years old. The younger generation contains more goethite than hematite, and reflects the change in local water composition at the time. Similar concretions have been found on Mars (the Mars Blueberries).

In the Hopi language, Moqui means "dear departed ones" or "the dead". The Hopi believe that the marbles are left behind each night by their

191

ancestors, who play with them at night and leave them to assure the living that all is well on the other side. Shamans of old used them to connect with the dead and extraterrestials, and to reach trance states. For healing, shamans would place the stone directly on the affected area of the body to remove dis-ease and control pain. A stone could also be held in each hand to calm and balance the client.

Moqui Balls are prized by many for their ability to help facilitate meditative states and trance journeys while still keeping one linked to their physical body. Due to their strong magnetic vibration, they present an ideal anchor to those who would travel between different planes of realities, so that one can easily return to one's body and time. Moqui Balls will raise the chi flow in the body and connect you to your higher self. Many people like to hold one in each hand as they perform spiritual work, or to grind two large ones together in one palm in meditation. Some people believe that there are male and female stones, and try to pair them together as such. You can sense the energies just by holding them, or by their appearance (often females may be more round, males more flat or with a central bulge, or females might be smooth vs. a male's roughness). Others believe female stones activate the higher chakras and portion of the body, and males energize the lower half.

Meditation with Moqui Marbles

Today we want you to rest. Just hold us, and rest. Relax your mind. Relax your muscles. Slow you breathing. Slow your body. Just rest.

Be easy.

Be restful.

Be open.

Are you ready? Open yourself to receiving, receiving the light of the universe and the light of your soul. Open yourself to the glow that surrounds you. You are a radiant, light being. Open yourself to your tru light. Open yourself to the truth of the universe. Take a few moments to bask in the radiance of your source...

Now, hold your stones in your hands, and open your self to their light. Feel the radiance and the energy that they bring as their auras mingle with yours. Hold your stones and welcome them. Take some time now to just relax and be with your stones. Allow yourself to be open and receive any messages they might have for you, and guidance or requests. Open, and receive.

You are whole, and you are blessed. Nothing but light surrounds you. Nothing but light is within you. You are a radiant, light being of love and joy. Take a deep breath, and return, here into your body, into your chair, in this room. Return.

Morganite

"Harness the healing power of love. This stone induces a warm a feeling of self-love all around you, and helps instill confidence and serenity in the bearer. It helps others to see you in the full light of your soul-ness, and enables you to do the same."

Morganite is a rarer member of the Beryl family, the same family as Aquamarine and Emerald. Beryls are beryllium aluminum silicates rich in minerals. Pure beryl is colorless. However, on account of its structure, it is in a position to intercalate foreign elements such as iron, manganese, chrome or vanadium. If manganese is intercalated in beryl, the rather plain, colorless gemstone turns into an enchanting pink treasure: Morganite.

Morganite as a stone is about love and trust - and as a crystal it is so intense in these feelings that you cannot help but say "yes" to it in each moment. It creates a sense of connection or closeness to the soul that not only allows us to experience that love that emanates from that part of us but also creates a sense of inseparability and permanence. It helps us see opportunities not barriers and teaches us that life is more about how we do things than what we do. In other words the answers and indeed the barriers are usually in the approach not in the actions and it is from this perspective that we need to deal with them.

This has an interesting impact in that often we doubt our own capacity or ability to do things, but with this connection to the soul and the wisdom of the soul we see ourselves differently and the obstacles we have placed in our own way appear to dissolve. The fragmentation we often create between different "selves" - the person you are at work, the one you are with your family, the spiritual person, etc., also dissolve as Morganite helps you be and express who we truly are. It reminds us that we don't need to try to be more or less than we are at the moment and that who we are is enough - in fact it's perfect. That is knowledge and awareness that only truly comes with seeing with the soul's eyes and truly loving and respecting who and what you are - and what you are here to do.

Morganite can also help us release the confusion about who we are supposed to be and the expectations placed on us. Similarly it can be used to release others from the expectations we may have of them -- granting them true freedom in our relationships.

As an extension of this theme, Morganite can be used to help heal feelings of abandonment and rejection - reminding us that we aren't alone and that we are forever supported by love. Similarly it can help overcome feelings of apathy, boredom and dispiritedness- because these are really just disconnection from the heart, and from love which causes our motivation levels to drop.

Morganite is known both as an angel stone and a heart stone. It can bring love to one's live or rekindle old love. As an angel stone, it is known to help with communicating with angels. Morganite also brings compassion, empathy, self-control, and patience. It can also balance emotions and ease the pain of separation. It has been said to be one of the highest frequency stones available.

Physically, Morganite is used for healing emphysema, tuberculosis, heart disease, breathing problems, and throat problems. Morganite is associated primarily with the heart and thymus chakras, and can open, balance and clear these chakras.

Meditation from Morganite

Be at peace. Hold your space. Close your eyes and relax your body, relax your mind, let go of the fear and the doubts. Hold your piece of Morganite tightly to your breast and breathe. Breathe in, and breathe out. I will help you see the way to clarity. I will help you see the way to love and no fear.

Breathe.

Just Breathe.

Feel the light of your soul radiating all about you. You are a perfect, radiant being. There is nothing about your life here on earth that is not perfect. There is nothing that you are doing wrong, nothing that you ever have done wrong, nothing that you ever could do wrong. All is perfection, for in your own perfection as part of source, how can you ever be wrong. Let your soul connect with your mind, with your physical body, and you will see with new eyes. You are just as you should be. Everything you are wanting to do now, to be next, is just as it should be. Do what you want. Be who you are. It is time. Now is the time.

I am Morganite, and I am here to support you. Let us begin. Hold me, feel me, and let us talk.

Now breathe. Breathe me into your body. We are as one, we will work as one to create your loving reality.

You are blessed in all things.

Go in Peace.

Nuummite

"Starchildren. Finally, you return. We watch you, we hear you, and now, you are beginning to hear us again, too. This stone you hold here is a communication stone, a means to contact we the races who seeded you there on Earth. Questions? We have many answers. We are mostly concerned with helping you to once again reach your fullest potentials, to raise your awareness and energies on earth so that you can emerge as a stronger, more compassionate race. We want your heart and souls to fly, and even your bodies. You have so many abilities you have yet to tap into. But the beginning has been made, and this stone here will lift you up further."

Nuummite is the oldest known mineral in existence at around 3 billion years old. It is a laminate mined north of Nuuk, Southern Greenland, in a high, difficult mountain terrain. It is volcanic in origin and its unique flasg derives from millennia of pressing and metamorphism.

Nuummite has called both the Sorcerers and Magician's stone. It has strong elemental properties that can awaken magical abilities in those who align with it. At the very least, it carries a high vibration that tends to catalyze spiritual growth and personal improvement.

It can help you access past lives and times well beyond modern history. It has a potent electro-magnetic field and many healers use it to help clear obstacles and energy drains from the physical, auric and etheric bodies. Because of this, nuummite is also helpful in recovering lost memories and helping us overcome limitations we have placed upon ourselves.

Nuummite is strongly shielding and grounding, making it a wonderful stone for protection and fortitude. It clears the aura and aligns the chakras on all levels.

When you work a lot with Nuummite, lucky coincidences increase and you often begin to lead a sort of charmed life. This is part of the magic it imparts – a natural side-effect of being in tune with your true self.

Meditation with Nuummite

Close your eyes and relax.

We're going to go back. Back in time, back in space, back to the beginning of who you are and what you do. Back to the origin of your now.

Count backwards, and relax your body, get really comfortable, and take nice deep breaths. Just relax and let go.

10.

9.

8.

7.

6.

5.

4.

3.

2.

1.

Just relax. You are here now, at the origin of your being. Let yourself explore and learn. Let the lessons begin.

SILENT MEDITATION

You are filled with the energy of source, filled and fulfilled. Your vibration is strong, pure and divine.

Now return back to the present here, at the count of three.

1.

2.

3.

Kunzite

"Kunzite is a master healer stone. It is one of the key stones for ascension into the New Age. Every color variation, every specimen, has something invaluable to teach you humans. Every piece no matter how small or imperfect will raise your vibration. Use it well, for that is the only way one can use Kunzite. No ill may come of this stone. No harm, no bad thought or feelings. Only love, compassion, gentle strength and healing."

Pink Kunzite is a powerful, high level stone. It is used against negative energy and anger because it empowers positive and loving thoughts. Most effective on the Heart Chakra , it opens the emotional heart and spiritual heart. It represents unconditional lovingness and compassion. Used for healing abuse/loss/addictions. Helps emotional balance, confidence, connection to higher self and oneness.

Kunzite is a stone that awakens the heart center. It produces loving thoughts and communication. It connects you to universal love and is beneficial to those who find it hard to meditate. Kunzite is also used on the Brow and Crown Chakra for the reason that it deepens altered states: psychic readings, healing...being centered emotionally and spiritually. Strengthens healers and teachers.

It is a protective stone that has the power to dispel negativity. It encourages self expression and allows free expression. It removes obstacles of life and helps to adjust to pressures of life. Promotes tolerance for the self and others. Helpful in reducing stress related anxiety, Kunzite is excellent for panic attacks. Used for calming epilepsy, soothing joint pain and stimulates the immune system. This crystal is recommended for reducing depression, mood swings, stress, radiation. Used extensively by the medical profession for psychiatric disorders. Good for the circulatory system and the lungs. A soothing stone that can help you adjust to the pressures of modern life.

Most often pink or clear in color (the green version is also called Hiddenite). Kunzite is a member of the Spudomene family that gets its color from manganese and lithium. Kunzite has been dubbed the evening stone due to the fact that it fades in bright sunlight. In addition to being pleochroic, it is sometimes phosphorescent.

Meditation with Kunzite

Close your eyes and relax. Take some nice, deep calming breaths and imagine that you are filled with a pretty pink light, easing through your cells and your body, suffusing your entire body, your entire being with peace and love, joy and ease. Allow this peaceful feeling to radiate out from all your chakras. Your root chakra. Your sacral chakra. Your solar plexus. Your Heart. Your Throat. Your Third Eye. Your Crown. See the pink light filling you, filling the room, filling the world. See everyone you love filled with the same pink light. See everyone, everywhere you went today, filled with pink light. See the cities around you filled with pink light. See New York, London, and Tokyo filled with pink light. See the world glowing pink from afar.

Now imagine that you are connected to everyone in this room by a stream of flowing energy, flowing in and out of your third eyes like a shining silver ribbon, flowing around the room in a circle. Feel the calming energy of Source entering you through the back of your head at the base of your skull, radiating through your body, and streaming out of you through the front of your forehead at your third eye. Feel the wonderful energy connecting each of you through your third eyes. Allow the love and connectedness to flow through your crown, your third eye, your heart and your soul. Feel the light and the love of Source, of the Holy Spirit, surround you. Know that you can feel this love and connection at anytime, with anyone.

You are whole, and you are blessed. Now focus on your stone. What would you like to say to it? What would it like to say to you? Does it have any messages, or a name? Spend some time now communing with your piece of Kunzite, with your piece of heaven.

Now focus your light and your love on your own being. Bring all your light into yourself. Bring your silver cord back into yourself. Call in your pink light, your love and your joy. Wrap yourself up in your love.

You are whole. You are one.

Return.

Pink Opal

"We are sweetness and joy, peace and happiness. There is little in this world that bothers us. We bring peace and understanding to all who work with us, we help heal rifts of misunderstanding and bring harmony to all situations."

Opal is a non-crystalline mineral formed of a combination of silica and water formed into a hardened gel. Most opals contain between 5 and 15% water by weight, although some contain even more. For this reason, opals should not be subjected to abrupt changes in temperature, which may cause them to crack, or extreme heat, which may cause them to dry out and crack.

In India, the opal was associated with the Rainbow Goddess, while in Arab nations it was believed to be an amulet of invisibility.

The silica structure of opal makes it an optimal stone of transformation for the new age as we evolve into crystalline beings. The water contained within allows us to transform old karma, emotional wounds and anger into wisdom, love and compassion. It helps us accept change gracefully and with ease, like a rock in a stream. They are also very good aids in meditation, astral travel, and work with the Akashic Records (ie: past life retrievals). It is believed by many that opal can help fight off depression and will strengthen one's will to live.

Pink opal is said to help smooth and heal the aura and work with the Akashic records to heal past traumas. Pink opal heals the heart, helps with dreaming and is known to be both uplifting and calming. It is an ideal stone to use during times of stress.

Traditionally, it has been used to strengthen love between those who are faithful. Physically, pink opal is said to improve the skin and help lessen the effects of diabetes (of course, because it reconciles us with the sweeter side of life).

All opals are traditionally believed to be stones of luck and good fortune. There is a newer, modern superstitions about opals as stones of misfortune, but these rumors originated from the gem industry's effort to sell more diamonds. Opals are wonderful wishing stones. They will project and magnify the emotions of the wearer and help to transform emotions and desires into concrete reality (make sure you are in a good state of mind when you work with opal!)

Meditation with Pink Opal

Hold opal in your heart and imagine yourself bathed in warm, pink light.

Imagine this light surrounding you, cleansing your aura and filtering through your skin, through your cells and organs, cleansing and revitalizing your cellular DNA.

Feel all your chakras flowing easily with energy, and your heart center expanding.

Now feel the spirit of the stone, the personality within the light. Hear the words of pink opal coming to you, engaging you. What messages does it hold for you today?

Allow yourself to quietly gather in the pink light of the stone, to pull it into your heart center, to fill your self up with the light.

You are joyful.

You are radiant.

You are filled with peace and harmony.

All is well.

Return.

Pumice

"Pumice strengthens your core. It builds strength in your body, courage in your heart, and enchances the connection between your mind and soul. It does not activate kundalini energy or the flow of source energy, it builds and improves the pathways upon which these energies travel, thus improving your life on Earth."

Pumice stone, or floating rock, is a special form of glass that is created when volcanos erupt. Lava is ejected, mixing with air and water to create a frothy foam which cools and depressurizes very quickly and hardens into pumice. Due to its frothy, sudden birth, pumice contains many holes formed from the bursting of gaseous bubbles, and is very light. It is so light, in fact, that some pieces can float on water – it has even been known to form the base of large floating islands or rafts which will travel for years along ocean currents.

Pumice is a common crystal, yet it possesses the rare qualities of the five elements -- earth, fire, water, air and ether. All are mixed together in this wonderful stone. Allow Pumice to walk with you and you will learn that spirit and body are one, and become more fully integrated and realized as a being of light. Pumice perfects the physical shell that houses your spirit. Pumice helps bring the messages of Source into the mind and body, so that it can be expressed for the highest good of all, without delay or confusion, but with perfect clarity and lightness of being.

Pumice opens the crown chakra and cleanses the meridians. It strengthens the skeleton and core of the body, so that Qi energy may flow better. It benefits both meditative and physical activities.

Pumice is used commercially as an abrasive cleanser – it can be used this way energetically, too, and is considered by many healers to be a wonderful "sponge" that will soak up and cleanse negative energy from the aura or a room. In this way, pumice opens up the emotional pathways to forgiveness and compassion, and can help ease pain, anger and sadness. Let pumice lift your spirits and improve your circumstances as it helps you help yourself.

Meditation with Pumice

Sit quietly, and feel your body. Feel the energy of spirit entering your crown chakra as ether, and blending with the air which enters in through your mouth, through your esophagus down to your lungs. Feel the air and ether lighting the fire in your solar plexus to fuel your blood as it travels through your veins, down through your arms and legs, to your feet and your hands, where it gathers the energy of earth, and returns your gut to blend with the energy of water, to nourish your body. Feel your body flowing and churning, feel the fire, the water, the earth, the air, the ether, that makes you, you. The elements that create your earthly shell are but divine components of spirit. They blend and mix together to create your earthly shell. They flow and they glow and they gather and disperse with each breath you take, each beat your heart makes, every pulse of each neuron in your brain, every moment each cell awakes.

You are alive. You are energized.

Now hold your pumice in your hand, and feel how it aligns with each element in your body.

Feel the Earth.

Feel the Water.

Feel the Fire.

Feel the Air.

Feel the Ether.

Now spend some time with your stone. How can it help you on your journey through life?

Hold your Pumice, and breathe into it.

Breathe out the negative patterns you've accumulated.

Breathe in the fresh power and energy of spirit.

Breathe out the old and stale.

Breathe in the fresh and pure.

Breathe in. Breathe out.

Return.

Rhodizite

"We seem so small, but we are huge, huge energy. We contain the power of the atom within us, the power of the tiny honeybee, the humming, buzzing energy of electricity, running through us, in us, around us. Use us to raise your energy. Use us to feel full of power and excitement. We could be bigger. Sometimes, on other planets, we are bigger. But here, if you were holding larger pieces of us, it would be overwhelming. We are just right. Let us fill you, full to overflowing, our energy will be yours and you will be unleashed."

Rhodizite is a complex form of borate that crystallizes in small 10-sided dodecahedrons and comes from Russia and Madascar. It has a long history of use by African shamans and medicine men.

Rhodizite is considered one of the most powerful healing crystals around, despite its small stature. It perfects the energetic blueprint of the body and crystal healers use it to clear cancer cells and repair DNA in the body. It is one of the few crystals that never need to be cleansed – it repairs and clears its own blueprint, too. Like pure Qi energy or reiki, it can be used to help the dying to clear blockages before they pass over.

Rhodizite increases energy in big, big ways. Use it to boost the immune system and instigate healing, or try it for manifesting your deepest desires. Wear it in a long medicine pouch around your neck, hanging low, so that its circular, spiraling energy can enter the body without overwhelming the upper chakras. Or try it with other crystals to activate and amplify their signals.

Rhodizite is aligned with the energy of our Sun, and sometimes it feels like they hold all the fusion power of that star right in their tiny matrixes. Allow Rhodizite to boost your strengthen your own inner-strength, release depression and past life blockages, and let your light shine!

Meditation with Rhodizite

Close your eyes, and think of the sun. Imagine that you are basking in the glow and the radiance of the sun, all the warmth and the power. You feel happy. You feel alive. You are surrounded by the energy of the sun, your auras mingle together, and you know, with every cell of your body, every fiber of your soul, that you are loved by the soul, that the sun cares for you, and that it fuels life on this planet in every way that you can conceive of. It is the source of everything, of all the life and the laughter and the love that dwells on earth. The fights we have over power, over who is right and who isn't, everything diminishes beside the power and the light of the sun. The sun is the only true power on earth. Without it, we are nothing.

Breathe in the energy of the sun, feel it welcoming you home. Feel the sun's rays like a kiss, the warmth like a womb. Slowly, the sun draws you in, draws you into its rays, into its womb. The sun coddles you, nourishes you, takes care of you. It is the power of love and creation, unleashed. You have your rhodizite crystal with you, and it feels like the sun in your hand, you feel the energies are harmonious, balanced and full of enthusiasm for whatever you need.

Take some time now to speak with the sun and your stone, to see how you might all work together, and how to plant the seeds for a successful, fulfilling life, how to love and laugh as naturally as you breathe, how to be the person you are meant to be. Take time now, with your star and your stone, and see.

Now thank your stone and thank the sun. Thank them for their support, for their love, for their energy. Step out of the light, out of the radiance, feel the warmth of the sun receding, while you take a little piece of it home with you, keeping a bit of that warmth and radiance in your solar plexus and in your stone.

Breathe in, and breathe out.

Breathe in, breathe out, and return. Return to this room, to this chair, to your body. Return.

Ruby with Kyanite

"Clear the path to universal Christ Consciousness. You have opened your hearts, now let us help you hollow them out, refresh them and make them as new and as pure as the heart of the universe. Let the center of your being being filled with the light of Source. We are here to help you be the true you."

Ruby and Kyanite together is a powerful combination that will help to bring dreams into reality while releasing old patterns that are not for our highest good. This stone can help reveal what one needs in order to stay balanced. Together they protect you from both physical and energetic negativity while surrounding you with peaceful vibrations allowing you to manifest your heart's desire.

The Ruby aspect in Kyanite acts as a nurturing stone with healing and positive effects on the emotions. It emanates protective energies, while shielding from negativity. Ruby helps us to see the true nature of love, and reveals the Divine Love in every thing in the Universe. Ruby is a stone which can enhance our courage and passion. It is said to initiate the kundalini and to increase one's supply of life-force energies. Ruby is often recommended for clearing root and heart chakra blockages.

Kyanite never needs cleansing due to the fact it constantly clears negative energy on all levels. The energy of kyanite is unlimited in application, making it one of the very best attunement stones. Kyanite aligns all the chakras automatically and immediately, with no conscious direction.

Kyanite brings tranquility and a calming effect to the whole being, with particular focus on the throat chakra and the third-eye. It stimulates communication and psychic awareness on all levels. It dispels anger and frustration and helps to facilitate clarity with respect to mental awareness and linear reasoning. Kyanite facilitates meditation and is quite useful when accessing the astral plane or connecting with ones guides. It provides for balancing of the yin-yang energies, bringing an orderly growth to the intellect, emotions and physical body.

Meditation with Ruby Kyanite

Tonight we want you to rest. We want you to hold us in your hands and just rest.

Rest, and release the pressures that are upon you.

Rest, and release the questions you have.

Rest, and release the energies you are holding which are not yours.

Let everything go. Just let it go, and feel yourself becoming more peaceful, more restful, more you.

Now sit quietly and let your thoughts flow. Feel how you are connected to everything, and how you are loved. We are here for you, with you, right here, right now. How can we best serve you?

You are open, and you are free. We are here for you. We support you.

You are loved, and all is well.

Awaken, and rejoice.

Selenite
(White Gypsum)

"Selenite was placed here on earth by the angels. It has been used by mankind for millennia to clear the burdens of physical being, to realign the spiritual being at the center of your body and to raise your vibration. It facilitates astral projection and allows the physical body to transcend your current earthly realm to reach higher dimensions."

Passed through the aura and around the body, selenite will cut cords and remove energy drains. Placed in a room it will clear geopathic and electromagnetic stress, as well as any other form of negativity. It is so good at clearing that the stone itself never needs to be cleansed, as it will never hold negative energy itself. Note: Do not wash or immerse selenite, it is water-soluble and will slowly degrade.

Selenite is a very calming and soothing energy. It's said to be the "Stone of mental clarity", enhancing mental flexibility and strengthening the ability to make good decisions. You can access information from past lives, using the energy of a Selenite wand. It is said to remove energy blocks from the physical and etheric bodies. It helps to connect the physical and etheric or 'light' bodies. Selenite wands can be used to clear other stones that are placed on or near it. Selenite is considered to be a 'mental body stone' which also opens, aligns and clears the aura bodies. It is able to transmit light, energy, and information; this maybe why many like to use it for channeling.

It can be used as a scanning device for those of us who are not visually orientated to get an overall view of a person's light system to see the thought forms in their energy body. You can direct the energy towards your client or yourself by physically pointing the Selenite towards your client and mentally aligning with its vibration to examine the thought forms that are stored within each energy body. From what I understand about Selenite wands it can be a powerful tool, but intent seems to be necessary in activating it. I personally like to use the Selenite wand when no other stones seem to be working.

Selenite is associated with the crown chakra and is used to decrease epilepsy and seizure disorders. It is also said to promote good business practices and would therefore excellent for any Healer, massage therapist, Reiki Master, Chiropractor, etc. to have in their office. It has been used by Healers to align the spine and is thought to be good for the skeleton and spine. It's also said to be an aid to help stop smoking.

Meditation with Selenite

Imagine you are walking down, deep into the earth. The tunnel is warm, but comfortable, and well lit. You feel excited and at ease as you progress downwards.

You emerge into a large cavern, filled with many vast pieces of Selenite. Some of the selenite beams lie across each other, and they are big enough for you to walk on, some of them measuring twenty, even thirty feet in length. You revel in the clarity of the energy here, and make your way towards a particularly smooth beam. You run your hands over the beam, feeling calm and clear, and you lie down on the beam.

Allow selenite to clear your aura and shift your energy away from negativity. Any attachments you have to other people that are depleting your energy are removed. You feel refreshed and rejuvenated.

When you are ready, thank the stones and return back through the tunnel, back into your room, into your body, knowing that you may return here as often as you wish, whenever you wish.

Septarian

"We are here to help you settle down. We want you to be happy with what you have, to integrate your dreams and your desires with your current reality. To help you cease your yearning and dissatisfaction, and see all the wonder that surrounds you, right here and now."

Septarian combines the calming, smoothing properties of yellow calcite, the grounding, cooperative properties of brown aragonite, and the cleansing influence of limestone. Overall, septarian is a very grounding stone which connects us with the Earth matrix of creation, promoting feelings of safety and easiness. It benefits all the lower chakras, strengthening the wearer against psychic attacks and negative emotional energies.

Septarian is very useful for those engaged in group activities or having difficulties in their inter-personal relationships. Septarian allows one to think problems through from beginning to end, and organize information in a more useful manner. The calcite helps one feel more patient and hear the other side of the story better, while the aragonite opens up positive pathways of communication, cooperation and co-creation. It is reputed to boost confidence while encouraging one's innate psychic abilities in order to help one anticipate and better cope with change.

The nurturing aspect of septarian extends into its powers of physical healing, soothing the body to aid muscle spasms, strengthening bones and cleanse the kidneys, liver and blood. Many people report feeling more physically energized when they use septarian, and it is often recommended to reverse the effects of chronic fatigue.

Septarian is widely believed to have formed from bentonite clay balls covered with decomposing seashells in the ocean during periods of volcanic activity 50 – 100 million years ago. Over time, the seashell solution mixed with the bentonite structure to crystallize into calcite, while the exposed areas of calcite further transformed into aragonite, and the outside of the septarian nodules became covered in limestone. The name septarian derives from the Latin word for divider or partition, "septum."

Meditation with Septarian

For this meditation, imaine your stone in your lap and breathe deeply, regularly.

Breath in and out.

In and out.

You hold the world in your hands, and the world flows and rises up to meet you. You have no boundaries. There is nothing holding you back. Everything in the world is created for you, by you, with you. You are the owner of your reality. Claim it.

Reach out for your stone. Gather it to you. Hold it to you. This is your dream. This is your creation. Hold it. Claim it.

Sit with your dream. Sit with your stone. Let your stone speak to you. You are now entering into a new era of co-creation and growth. Let it flow from your fingertips to your heart to your soul. Let it flow.

Now gather in your thoughts. Relax your mind. Thank your stone.

It is time to return.

You are here, you are blessed, you are now.

Return.

Shungite

"We are immortal. We are shungite. We hold old, old knowledge. That which you have hidden away or try to deny we can see, we know. Would you like to see what is hidden? We can help you with that. Let us help clear out the cobwebs, bring the darkness to light, and illuminate your being, your life, your world."

Shungite is one of the oldest minerals in the world, contains almost every element in the period table and is noted for its unique carbon structure. It is known to exist only in Karelia, Russia, near Shunga lake, and is about 2 billion years old. Scientists argue over whether it was formed volcanically, from primitive microscopic organisms or via meteorite impact. It's appearance is similar to coal, but its age predates almost all life on earth and therefore other coal formations. It has been used for decades in Russia with verifiable scientific proof that it cleanses impurities and radiation from water and increases the bioavailability of water to the body. It has been shown that shungite has both filtrative and antibacterial action and is biologically active. It is said to cleans water of various chlorine compounds, nitrates, copper, magnesium, and iron while enriching the water in potassium. Stones used in water enhancement should be cleansed by sunlight on a weekly basis and replaced every 6 months.

"Shungite cures, rescues, purifies, heals, protects, normalizes, restores and even stimulates the growth. Amazing rock: it kills and devours anything that harms people and other living beings, and concentrates and restores all that is good. The scholars who have studied shungite in one voice declare, it is a miracle! " -- From the book by A. Doronina "Shungite - the stone-savior"

The majority of Shungite's healing power comes from its carbon components, fullerenes. American scientists identified the unique fullerenes in Shungite which have implications for nanotechnology and cancer therapies, amonth other applications, and received a Noble Prize for this discovery. Fullerenes infused in water enter our bodies and become extremely powerful antioxidants. Shungite enhanced water has also been show to greatly decrease the activity of histamines in the bloodstream, thereby reducing inflammation and helping those who suffer from allergies. Fullerenes are being researched by many manufacturers for their potential applications, including UV skin protection, solar arrays, radiation treatments, asthma treatments and nanotechnology.

Metaphysically, shungite is believed to work on all levels of your being -- the spiritual, mental, emotional, and physical bodies – and clear out all harmful elements. Shungite takes issues which are lurking in the etheric and astral planes and brings them to light, facilitating personal growth and enlightenment. It is extremely protective and lends feelings of safety to all those who work with it. Need a shield? Employ shungite.

Meditation with Shungite

Let yourself relax into your body. Slow your breathing, sink down into your body. Breathe in, and feel your consciousness expanding deep within yourself, down, down into the darkness of your root chakra, deep into the earth, down into the center of your world.

Relax, and be easy. Be easy, and be whole. Be whole, and know that you are a pure vessel of light, deep in the darkness, there you are, full of light. There is nothing but light. Let your light surround you, let it glow, and let it flow.

Imagine you hold a piece of shungite to your body, hold it to the center of your light, wherever your light shines through the brightest. Hold this piece of god-force in your hand and let the light of the world, the light of you, fill you and illuminate all your being. Connect with the god-force and hear the truth of your life, a message meant just for you.

You are whole, you are held in the esteem of all the universe, uplifted by the wings of the angels, and you are loved.

Gather your light in, hold it deep to yourself, and know that you can always, any time, reveal your light to the world. The light is always for you, with you, of you.

Return now, and be of the light.

Sunstone

"We are the warm fire of creative potential, that is why we are called sunstone. We glow with possibilities, we bring you the anticipation and excitement associated with new projects, new growth. Use us to fuel your passions to birth a better life experience."

Like Labradorite, Sunstone is a variety of plagioclase feldspar that contains orange and gold flash emanating from red hematite, as if it holds the sun inside it. It forms in magma, cooling in deposits formed via volcanic activity. Some of the most valuable, more translucent sunstone comes from Norway and the United States in Oregon (where it has copper inclusions instead of hematite). It is also common in North America, India, Russia and Madagascar.

Sunstone has always been associated with luck and prosperity. It is a strengthening stone, work with the second and third chakras to alleviate fear and bring joy and light into our lives. It boosts self-confidence and helps change "poor-me" or victim attitudes so that the person can begin to stand up for themselves and live the life they are meant to. Perhaps because of this, sunstone is believed to encourage self-healing and boost the immune system. Use it to call in the light and clear any chakra while strengthening the aura, or to encourage a "sunny" disposition and fight depression. Many people use sunstone to alleviate pain, whether they have a sore throat, damaged cartilage or a bad back.

Use it with moonstone on solstices to honor the Sun and Moon, and balance yin and yang energies (sunstones are considered yang, masculine stones.) Sunstones are filled with positive, impassioned energy, and may boost sexual energy or help breathe new life into a stale relationship. It is associated with fire energy and the sun sign Leo.

Sunstone can also be used to cleanse negative emanations from the biofield, much like selenite, by "smudging" the body with the stone. This will remove cords of attachment from other people that may be causing energy drains in your body.

Meditation with Sunstone

Close your eyes and relax. Lift your head to the sky, and imagine that the sun is beating down on you, warm, reassuring, gentle. Imagine that it is a perfect fall day, not too cold, not too warm, sunny with a light breeze ruffling through the yellow and orange autumn leaves. The sun beats down on your face, and you feel blessed to receive the glowing energy from its rays, filled with the love and the light of source, fueling vitamin D production in your body and boosting your immune system. You sit in the sun and you feel warm, healthy and revitalized.

Hold your stone in the palms of your hands and let it soak in the sun's rays, too. Allow the sun to fully awaken your crystal. Feel the stone turning warm in your hand, alive and intelligent.

Now hold your stone to your forehead, to your third eye. Feel your mind connecting to the life force inside the stone person you hold. Ask it what it would like to be called, if it has a name for you to know, and if there are any messages for you that it would like to share. How can you best align with the energy of sunstone?

The sun is beginning to fade now, to set behind the trees and mountains. Gather up the last of its rays upon your face, and thank your stone for her knowledge and wisdom. Ask how you can best host the stone in your home and your life. Does it have any favors to ask of you?

The sun has set. Hold your stone in your hands and thank it again. Thank the sun and the fire of the earth for bringing sunstone to you. Breathe in, and breathe out. And Return.

Tangerine Aura Quartz

"Tangerine Aura quartz connects you to solar energy in a real and tangible way. It will boost vitamin production in the body and helps you to process and assimilate nutrients more efficiently. It brings in joy and light to the body, through the crown chakra and the diaphragm, so that you become energized, potentized, awakened. Stronger. When you work with any aura quartz, you are consciously creating a connection between your present reality and the technological mysteries of your ancestors, because you are using technologies to enhance your crystals in powerful ways which your present scientists are only just beginning to understand."

Tangerine Aura Quartz (also called Melon Quartz, Imperial Gold Aura or Tangerine Sun Aura Quartz) is natural clear quartz whose color has been altered through an application of vaporized Gold and Iron Oxide under intense heat in a vacuum, which permanently bonds the metals to the quartz crystal's surface. Copper is also added sometimes to the mix of gold and iron oxide.

Holding a similar vibration to tangerine quartz, tangerine aura quartz can be used to strengthen the sacral chakra while it helps connect and clear all the lower chakras. It is great for combating issues of self-worth so that one can find and claim their rightful place in the world. Not sure what to do today, or where your headed in life? Try carrying a piece of Tangerine Aura -- it allows your body to sense the way, to unite guidance from your soul with direction from your mind.

Tangerine Aura stabilizes the emotions and can also be used to unleash creativity. This is a wonderful stone for working on manifestation and the law of attraction.

Physically, it can be helpful to boost sexual energy or heal sexual organs. Many healers also use tangerine aura quartz to improve digestion and elimination, stimulate the appetite or encourage weight loss, regulate blood sugar and energize the body.

Meditation with Tangerine Aura Quartz

Imagine the stone at your diaphragm and breathe.

Breathe in, and breathe out. In and out.

Imagine a sunny orange glow coming from your stone, radiating out into your hands, into your abdomen, into your body, growing brighter and larger as you breathe in, and you breathe out.

Feel the orange light flowing through your belly, up into your solar plexus and your lungs, up through your arms and your head. Feel it flowing down, too, down through your hips, into your legs, through your knees and your calves, down into your ankles, your feet, your toes. Feel the orange light flowing freely through your body, dissolving blockages and repairing cells as it flows past them, through them, around them. Feel your body growing energized. You feel stronger. You are stronger. You feel alive. You are alive.

Now, imagine yourself sitting in a beautiful place, the sun beating down on you. You are warm. You are radiant. You are surrounded by life, blessed by our great central sun. You feel wonderfully alive. What will you do now? How will you put your new energy to use? Spend some time now, relaxing in the sun, and ask your stone for guidance, see if it has any special messages for you.

The sun is beginning to set, it's beautiful golden rays turning magenta and deeper orange. Thank the sun for its warming energy, and thank your stone for its messages. You feel whole, you feel blessed. You feel relaxed and happy.

Breathe in.

Breathe out.

Breathe in.

And out.

It's time now to return, leaving the setting sun behind, and return back into this room, into your body, right here, here and now.

You are blessed. Return.

Tanzanite

"Tanzanite soothes and illuminates. It lifts the veil from the eyes so that the soul can shine through, and the mind can see what is really there in front of it, growing, shifting, happening. It brings you more fully into the moment but removes all sense of urgency and worry. With Tanzanite, you can just be."

Tanzanite comes from Tanzania, where it was discovered in the shadow of Mount Kilamanjaro in 1967. It is a type of Zoisite related to Epidote. It contains vanadium, which creates its unique periwinkle hue when the stone is heated (whether naturally in the earth or by man). Tiffany's held exclusive rights to the sale of the stone for a long time, having discovered and owned the original mines. It is becoming increasingly rare, since most mines in Tanzania are nearing depletion. At different angles, a piece of tanzanite may appear different hues, ranging from gray to blue to lavender. Warmer lighting also enhances the lavender color.

Tanzanite has a calming quality that helps people take a step back from the chaos of modern daily life and relax a little. Many people refer to it as the "workaholic's stone." It is wonderful at helping one create more harmony and balance between all aspects of one's life. Tanzanite allows to self-actualize all aspects of our self, so that we can overcome repressed fears and release blocks or personal conflicts.

Tanzanite activates and connects the upper chakras, from the heart to the throat to the crown to source. It is said to enhance spiritual insight, making it an ideal companion during meditation. Use it to help bring about alignment with Source energy and one's own higher self.

Physically, Tanzanite may be used to help with high blood pressure, migraines, inflammation, and general stress, depression or panic issues. Bringing one more into balance with one's true self, tanzanite helps return the body to optimum performance, enhancing cellular renewal, immunity, detoxification, and metabolic performance.

Note: If Tanzanite leaves you feeling spacey, keep a grounding stone like carnelian or onyx handy to activate your lower chakras, creating a balance of the upper and lower realms in the body.

Meditation with Tanzanite

Close your eyes and relax.

Envision tanzanite in both hands and feel its energy traveling your arms, through your shoulders and throat chakra, and spreading down through your heart chakra. Feel this energy fueling a violet flame within your heart center. The violet light grows and radiates, glows and expands. It consumes all negativity in its path as it radiates through your body, up to your crown chakra and down through to your toes. The light is like a flame, transforming damaged cells and repairing DNA in your physical body. See your body returning to a perfect state of self-renewal and health. See your body as the perfect vehicle for your soul. Your soul created and approved this body for its use. It loves this body. Feel the love and acceptance flow through you, from you. You are perfection. You are love. You are at peace.

Now see the violet fire expanding through your crown chakra and connecting to your true self.

See your higher self feeling energized and and excited by the balanced light emanating from your body. You are fully at one with your self. You are exactly the you that your soul has been wanting.

All is well. Now allow the violet fire to subside, infusing yourself and your surroundings with a quiet glow of health and ease. Open your self now to your stone, who is here to help and nourish your being with love and acceptance. Take this time now to communicate and receive any messages your stone might have for you.

Now thank your stone, and welcome it into your life.

You are whole.

You are blessed.

All is well.

Gather in your aura and your energies, and allow your soul to inhabit your body at its full potential. Return to your body. Return to the room. Wiggle your toes and rub your stones.

You are here.

You are blessed.

Tibetan Tektite

"These Tektites are very special. Tektite is always grounding and calming, a gift from above to connect you to the creative intent of your Planet. They can help you connect to your inner resources, and help you tap into all your true power and energies. Tektite from Tibet also carries the resonance of mantras, meditations and prayers that have been sung in that land for centuries. It carries some of the highest spiritual evolutionary energies on your Earth, and thus help you tap into your highest potentialities."

Tektites are suspected of being of meteoric origin and can be used for star magic. They are rich in silica similar to natural glass (obsidian). It is found in oval or elongated forms with very pitted surfaces. This pitting suggests that the stone was cooled under water adding the water element of cleansing to the overall energy. At a glance it looks black in color. But a close look at the edges reveals it to be a dark golden yellow. Tektite has the healing characteristics of a stone native to Earth with a slightly different feel when used in meditation. Many find this difference manifests itself by providing a much larger view of an issue than what appears on the surface.

Tektites are protective in nature and it is protective against fire and storms if buried near your front and back doors. It aids one in grounding into Earth reality, so can also be used as an abundance charm. They are said to activate the third eye, assists one in visionary work, as well as assisting in both lucid dreaming and dream recall. It will help you to make change by giving you the strength to do so. It strengthens the energy field and helps awaken kundalini while opening and clearing the lower chakras.

More than 2000 years ago, the Chinese referred to tektites as Inkstone of the Thundergod. Australian aborigines refer to them as Mabon, or 'magic' and believe that finding one brings good luck. In India, they are known as the Sacred Gem of Krishna. They assist one in attaining knowledge and learning lessons throughout the travels of life.

Because it can stimulate thought transmissions, meditation with a tektite will increase telepathy. Its vibrational energies have been known to heighten the awareness of its wearers, often by enhancing psychic sensitivity, clairaudient experiences and increasing the frequency of synchronicities in their lives. Many report having the experience of "seeing through the veil" of the physical world more readily with Tektite. It makes the hidden, deep truth obvious.

Meditation with Tektite

Relax. Breathe deeply and let the energies of the day go.

Let it all go.

Relax.

Feel your body relaxing, sinking into your chair, into the earth, into the deep dark womb of the Earth. Feel yourself easing into the womb of the Great Mother Earth. Feel the safety of the Earth around you, feel her heartbeat thrumming around you, hear the messages of the Great Mother sounding around you.

Listen to the Earth. Listen to the messages she has for you. Relax and allow her energies to fill and heal you.

Now allow your consciousness to shift to your tektite. Allow yourself to feel the difference of its energies. Welcome it into your presence. Does your stone have any messages for you, any special gifts of healing or intentions? Does it have a particular name it would you to call it by? Sit now with your stone and meditate with it.

Now gently return your consciousness to your body. Thank the Mother Earth for her blessings, and let your stone know that you will be working with it regularly over the coming weeks. Feel your body rising back up through the earth, back into the room, and into your chair. Feel yourself blessedly awake, fully alive, healed and energized, ready for tomorrow.

You are blessed.

You are well.

Tiger Iron Skull

"Are you ready to tap into all your strengths? Are you ready to be the true powerhouse of creation and decision that you are? Are you ready to stop being bombarded by negative vibrations and begin having great days? Every day? Well, that is what we are here to help you with. We harness the power of gold and silver, the sun and the mirror, the light and the shield. We bring these powers straight into your being, into your blood, to become one with you. Talk to us, and we will talk to you. We will help show you the way to security and joy that you desire. We will light the fire in your soul. Do not be afraid. There is nothing to fear about this process. It will be easy. It will be great."

Tiger iron, also known as Mugglestone, blends the properties of three stones: hematite, red jasper, and golden tiger's eye.

Hematite is best known for its emotionally protective qualities. It helps protect us from absorbing the negative emotions of others. Hematite, which helps to deepen the connection between spirit and body, grounds us in our sense of self and purpose. It is also a stone of clarity, particularly clarity of knowledge, enabling one to see the truth below the apparent surface of issues.

Considered in some Native American cultures to be the symbolic blood of the earth, Red Jasper quietly grounds us by connecting us to the deep, stabilizing energies of the earth. It's an emotionally calming stone and can be an excellent one for those who like change to be a gradual, unfolding process. With stabilizing effects, it can help people to be less susceptible to the emotions of others, thus enhancing the effects of hematite. It is a grounding stone that also brings protection, especially protection from danger.

Patience and a sense of timing are other aspects of grounding which relate to our ability to live with appreciation and joy on the earth plane. Many believe our purpose in being here is to translate nonphysical energy into the realization of our dreams. Tiger's eye helps us in this purpose. It specifically assists us by helping us to have more confidence in our ability to realize our dreams through the recognition of the inner resources we can use for accomplishment.

Tiger Iron also helps with creative endeavors and all types of artistic abilities. It is an excellent stone for people wishing to bring more motivation to their lives, and is a stone of good luck. In folklore and crystal healing lore, Tiger Iron is said to balance white and red blood cells, increase natural steroids, and improve muscular structure, and help with healing legs, sexual organs, liver, and the nervous system. Tiger Iron is related to the sacral and root chakras. Reach for it when you're feeling vulnerable, when your self-esteem has slipped, when your dreams seem unreachable. With tiger iron as your companion, you can learn to tread through life with strength, power, certainty, vitality, balance and grace.

Crystal skulls are tools of awareness. They help one focus, reflect, refract, amplify, attune, transmit, transform and store energy. They can also act as a witness to acts of intention. They tend to hold and store energy from other eras and dimensions with more clarity than other crystals. Do not be surprised when your skull begins talking to you – this is a common phenomenon, often beginning with an introduction and a name. There are ancient legends from around the world detailing the existence of 12 or 13 life-size crystal skulls which were pure crystal, had moveable jaws and were said to sing and speak when activated together. They are believed to have been ancient computers and are said to hold the knowledge of the origins and destiny of the human race. Legend says that when mankind has once again reached a certain level of consciousness or when the ley lines and energies of the Earth have been sufficiently healed, that these skulls will once again be reunited. All crystal skulls are believed to tap into the knowledge and powers of the ancient skulls, including the original 13, often called the "Atlantean Skulls". Many great civilizations believe there were 12 planets which were inhabited by humans and these souls could travel inter - dimensionally around them. Each planet was said to have a crystal skull and body belonging to them, which in turn has connections to different portals at various sacred sites around the earth.

To date there are some discrepancies as to how many of the Atlantean skulls have been discovered. However the most famous discovery of all was in 1924 by Dr Mitchell-Hedges and his daughter Anna at Lubaantum in British Honduras, better known today as Belize. When Anna passed away at the age of 100 in April 2007 she chose Bill Homan to be the guardian of this skull and here it remains for safe keeping.

When finding a crystal skull to work with, consider it a joint effort as the crystal skull also chooses you as their guardian. We feel attracted to a crystal skull because it has a vibration that we can resonate with and is compatible with our own unique vibration.

When you connect with a crystal skull it vibrates a stronger energy field, it calls to the person whose energy induces its activation through his or her resonance with that crystal skull.

Being a keeper or guardian of a skull is a wonderful experience. They will fill your life with fun, healing and excitement, you may be guided to travel to certain places to meet like-minded people and to work with earth healing. They will enhance your spiritual development and will be great teachers. If you open your heart to your skull it will become a great friend and will share information and healing energy with you.

Connecting with a
Tiger Iron Skull

Let's begin with a grounding exercise. Sit quietly, with your feet on the floor and imagine your roots growing from the bottom of your feet, going deep into the earth, down through the mud and the rocks and the water tables and down into the center of Mother Earth. Feel the connection. Ask that the earth to help you connect to Source or your angels and guides. See yourself safe and protected.

Now, hold your crystal skull in one or both hands in front of your heart chakra.

Connect to a feeling of unconditional love in your heart. Send this love and joy to the crystal. Ask that the crystal skull be cleared of any old programming and that it works for the light for the highest good of all.

Invite it to work with you in the future for healing and mediation.

Invoke the Angels, Ascended Masters, Mayan Lords of Light and the Ancient Keepers of the crystal skulls to activate your crystal skull. Ask and set the intent that it be connected to the ancient singing crystal skulls and the talking crystal skulls, and that they all be activated and connected to each other to heal the earth.

Once you have activated your skull if you wish you can ask it what planet or star system it connects to and what portal it resonates with. Then during meditation you may set the intent that it heals and activates that portal or sacred site.

Sit in quiet contemplation for a while, at this point you may be given the name of your skull and trust the first thing that comes into your mind.

If you do not hear the name, know that this will be revealed at the divine right time.

Close your meditation with the skull by thanking it for sharing its energies with you. Thank your guides and all who lent their presence to your meditation. Feel your feet on the floor and envision your roots returning back up through the earth, through the mud and the rocks and the waters, back up through the floor, retracting into your body. Take three deep breaths and feel the energy of the room flowing through your lungs, through your body.

Open your eyes.

You have returned.

Titanium Flame Aura Quartz

"We hold the line. We defend against the dark and ignite a fire within the soul so that one can return to the light. We bring in all the light and fire of creation. We hold the highest spectrum of reality within us, the rainbow of divinity. With us, you can truly shift into who you need to be, to be your best. There is no possibility of failure with us. Only light. Only divine miracles."

Titanium Flame Aura Quartz (also called Flame Aura, Titanium Aura or Rainbow Aura) is natural clear quartz whose color has been altered through an application of vaporized titanium molecules under intense heat in a vacuum, which permanently bonds the metals to the quartz crystal's surface.

Titanium Flame holds a vast amount of Qi energy. When held, it connects and clears all the chakras and stimulates kundalini in the body. This removes energetic blockages and allows the physical body to channel the will of the higher self, fast-tracking evolution and manifestation ablilities. It is, in every sense, a real power stone.

Titanium Flame can help you unleash your creativity or reach higher states of consciousness. If you tend to have a hard time reading people or situations, try carrying this stone with you – it can help you receive more accurate guidance from higher realms, and a better sense of true knowing. It transmutes negative, dark energy into positive, loving energy.

Physically, titanium quartz is a wonderful healing stone. It helps the central nervous system and spine, improving the immune system and the meridians. Benefits the head, eyes and ears.

Meditation with Titanium Flame Aura

Close your eyes and relax. Breathe in, and breathe out.

Allow your mind to wander, allow your muscles to just be, while you breathe in, and breathe out. Feel how good it is to just sit, and breathe, to just sit, and be.

Now, hold your stone in your hand, and feel the heat of it warming you gently. Feel the heat traveling up your arms, through your body, flowing through you while you continue to relax and breathe. It's just you and the stone, just the stone and you. You are one with each other and one with the divine light of source as you flow together through the universe. You are one with the light.

Now, what knowledge does your stone have for you today? What have you always known that could help you now. What have you always known that could change your life today if you let truth into your life? Your stone and you are one – what knowledge do you share? Spend some time now with your stone, and see what you have always known. Bring that knowledge to you, into you, so that you can transform your life for the highest good.

All is well. Thank your stone now, and gather in your energy. Bring the knowledge you have received with you, safe and bright, back into this world for the light of all.

Return to the room, to your body, and be well.

Return.

Topaz

"Topaz is a very high energy stone. It is similar to quartz in its healing potentials and versatility, but its energies are much, much more potent and focused. The vibrational powers of topaz shoot directly to the core of the physical and spiritual bodies, blasting through any barriers or indifferences. Topaz is perfectly aligned with gridwork because it can be charged for any purpose, regardless of its color, and once it is charged to a specific purpose it energies are unrelenting until its goal is reached. Topaz is strong, empowering and of the highest vibration. Are you ready?"

Natural topaz crystal has the energy of soft, warm encouragement. It belongs to the orthorhombic family of crystals, along with peridot and alexandrite. As a group, these are stones of greater perspective. Topaz is one of the hardest minerals, and is the hardest silicate mineral found in nature. A silicate of aluminum, topaz contains about 20 percent water and fluorine. The relative proportions of these impurities are responsible for the color of the stones. Crystals with more water are yellow to brown, while those with more fluorine are typically blue or colorless.

The properties of topaz instill a generous, empowered vision, attracting both joy and abundance in life. Topaz is also beneficial for physical healing, having a stimulating, encouraging influence over the body. The different colors of these crystal healing stones — clear, blue, golden, or pink — carry their own special properties as well.

In crystal healing, topaz is an incredibly positive stone. It helps one clearly see the way things are, helping to dispel falsehoods and bring about truth. Negative emotions such as doubt, uncertainty, and disillusionment are dissolved with the presence of natural topaz, and in fact, are transformed into feelings of trust and confidence. These positive vibrations help to bring about spiritual and psychological wealth. Some say a topaz crystal can even help physically manifest desires. This connection with abundance also encourages an individual to want to share and spread what knowledge, energy, or material that they may have.

For creative people having trouble realizing their worth, topaz will shed light upon an awareness of how valuable their work is. It also encourages an understanding of how the finer details in life are integrated with the purpose of the whole. Topaz crystals have a calming effect, allowing for inspiration and creative flow, as well as a greater spiritual connection. This stone is believed to cleanse, realign, and motivate the meridian system and the chakras, bringing about a powerful state of energetic balance. To use topaz for healing the mind and spirit, wear a topaz ring on the ring finger, or use in meditation, placing on the brow chakra.

The ancient Greeks believed that the fiery crystal had the power to increase a person's strength and make its wearer invisible in times of emergency. Topaz was also said to change color in the presence of poisoned food or drink. The gem's mystical curative powers waxed and waned with the phases of the moon. When the powdered stone was mixed with wine, it was considered a cure for asthma, insomnia, burns and hemorrhages. Some scholars trace the origin of the word topaz to the ancient Sanskrit word for fire, or tapas, a reference to its fiery orange color. These colors can change when exposed to sunlight and/or heat. Brown topaz can be bleached by sunlight and yellow topaz turns pink to purple-red when exposed to moderate heat. The latter phenomenon was discovered in 1750 by a Parisian jeweler who used it to create the first artificial pink topaz. Nearly all the pink topaz sold as jewelry has been heat-treated.

Meditation with Topaz

Breathe deeply. Relax you mind, your body, your soul. Imagine that you are inside a warm, cozy house, surrounded by light and love. You are comforted. You are relaxed. You are happy and full of easy thoughts.

There is a box in front of you on a table, covered with beautiful designs and colors, and you open the box. Inside, you find a handful of stones, and an piece of paper with a design that you can use to improve your physical reality on earth. You take the stones, and lay them on top of the paper, and feel the room fill with light. You are surrounded by radiant joy and light, laughter bubbles forth from your soul and you are happy.

You sit like this, with your stones, allowing your soul to fill with the light and energy of source.

All is well.

You return the stones to your pocket, and return here, to this room, to your body.

All is well.

Tourmaline

"Raw black tourmaline is filled with pure, raw warrior enegy. Not the angry warrior or the destroying warrior – tourmaline is the warrior of truth, the warrior of the people. It is the stone designated by the angels for protecting humanity on earth. It is the stone to turn to when you are overwrought, feeling torn down or beset from all sides. It is the stone to turn to when you are feeling wounded and unable to stand up for yourself anymore. It is the stone to turn to when you feel the world crumbling around you. Turn to tourmaline, and feel your worldview uplifted, feel what it is like to not worry, to not fear or cringe. Tourmaline is here for you. Use it!"

Tourmaline is a crystalline boron silicate mineral. Black tourmaline, also known as schorl, gets its color and strength from iron. Tourmaline is pyroelectric, and can attract and repel hot ashes. Egyptian legend holds that tourmaline is the "stone of the rainbow", because as it came to earth it passed through a rainbow and assumed all its colors.

Tourmaline is a high energy stone that is quite soothing and positive in nature. It seems to be especially concerned with helping humanity evolve, and so will often allow you to get to the root of problems and negativity. When you use tourmaline in this way, it also helps you attain greater compassion and understanding, so that true healing may occur.

Black tourmaline is an exception grounding stone with high vibrations, and shields the wearer from negativity of all kinds, including electromagnetic waves and radiation. Some of my favorite tourmaline specimens for grounding consist of the black rods at least the size of one's pinkie finger growing through clear or white quartz – they have a wonderfully clean effect on illnesses and the environment. It draws earth energy through the root chakra to increase one's vitality and energy.

Connecting with Tourmaline

The most powerful thing you can do to connect with Tourmaline is to drum. Regular heartbeat drumming will ground you and connect you to the full power of the stone as you envision its beautiful deep blackness. Drum for 10-30 minutes and see where the stone takes you.

Don't have a drum? That's okay! Buckets or pots beaten with a wooden spoon can work equally well, even a strong cardboard box.

Violet Obsidian

"We are the dream keepers, the holders of visions. We are the ones to call upon when your resolve is faltering, the ones to help you stay on your path. We are strength, we are beauty. We will help you to walk in the light and find your truth. There is nothing you can't do, there is no place you can't go or no one you cannot become. We are the dream keepers. Keep on keeping on."

Obsidian is a semi-precious gemstone created by lava that has surfaced from a volcano or lava stream and cooled off extremely quickly, so it has a beautiful glossy, glassy look to it. Obsidian is made from silicon dioxide and while it was used in the past for weapons and tools, today, it is mostly used for beautiful ornamental jewelry. Since Obsidian forms in many regions and can combine many minerals and elements, there are plenty of different varieties of Obsidian which are extremely unique and attractive. Obsidian can come in many different colors including dark green, dark brown, black, golden sheens, beautiful yellows, blues and purple. It often contains tiny air bubbles, sometimes giving it either a golden, green sheen or a rainbow sheen.

Violet Obsidian is a rare and beautiful variety of Obsidian that has the cooling properties of the Third Eye, Crown and Transcendental Chakra energies. This is a stone that shows us the power of spirituality and the endless possibilities through Universal attraction, love and growth. This stones connects us to our intuition, our auras fields and is one of the most powerful gazing stones for it comes from the earth, yet has the properties of the heavens. Clears the crown chakra, stimulates psychic awareness, dream recall and understanding. Brings clarity to past life relationships and also helps to clear karmic cords. It enhances spiritual growth and spiritual awareness while strengthening clairvoyance and introspection. The bond between intellect and intuition are reinforced.

Obsidian is a very grounding and healing stone, and is excellent for removing negativity no matter what its color. It is excellent protection against psychic attacks. In particular obsidian protects the gentle from abuse. Obsidian is also an excellent manifestation stone since it is aligned with the energies of fire and creation. It sharpens and focuses internal and external vision, and helps get in touch with buried issues before they explode.

A stone of honesty, sincerity and truth, obsidian will bring out the Warrior spirit in you. It can help reach into your subconscious, reclaim yourself, and help you find or re-discover forgotten abilities within yourself. Obsidian is an "ego buster" - reveling the truth about ourselves in a none too gentle manner. Obsidian cuts through all our defenses and exposes us naked to ourselves.

Meditation with Violet Obsidian

Close your eyes. Relax. Feel the your stone in your less dominant hand and relax. Feel the coolness and the heat within the stone. All obsidian carries both the cooling currents of air and the creative passions of Mother Earth within it, and you can use these energies to keep your focus while pursuing your own passions.

Feel the coolness. Feel the heat. Feel your spirit rising on warm currents of air into the sky, surrounded by refreshing clouds and vapors. You feel safe. You feel fresh and clear and clean. You are float on low-lying clouds above a rain forest, and you are filled with the clean, healing air gifted to you by the trees below.

Breathe it in. Breathe deeply.

Relax.

See your cloud infusing with the color of your stone, see the lavender and violet hues surrounding you. Quiet your mind. Let your worries go.

What would you like to ask your stone? What are your current concerns on your path?

Your stone has a message for you. Listen well.

Breathe deeply.

Breathe deeply.

Breathe in the air. Feel the energies of creation filling you, nourishing you.

All will be well. You are the master of your domain.

Breathe in the air.

Now feel yourself gently floating back down into your body, down. Down. Down. Into your body, into your seat. Down. Down. Into your legs. Into your knees. Into your toes. Down.

Down.

You have returned.

YELLOW & WHITE KUNZITE

"Kunzite is a master healer stone. It is one of the key stones for ascension into the New Age and will eventually be used by humans in technological applications, for kunzite allows the transfer of energy and information at an incredibly high rate. Every color variation, every specimen, has something invaluable to teach you humans. Every piece no matter how small or imperfect will raise your vibration. Use it well, for that is the only way one can use Kunzite. No ill may come of this stone. No harm, no bad thought or feelings. Only love, compassion, gentle strength and healing."

Most often found in stores in pink, green or purple, Kunzite comes in many color variations. Kunzite has been dubbed the evening stone due to the fact that it will fades in bright sunlight. In addition to being pleochroic, it is sometimes phosphorescent.

Kunzite is a powerful, high level stone. It can be used to dispel anger and rage, and bring in love, light and laughter. It awakens the heart center and encourages loving thoughts and communication. Try wearing it if you are having a hard time being supportive or nurturing, or if you are experiencing heartache or loss of a loved one. It connects you to universal love, and is even beneficial to those who find it hard to meditate. Kunzite is also used on the Brow and Crown Chakra for the reason that it deepens altered states: psychic readings, healing...being centered emotionally and spiritually.

Kunzite is a great stone for children or adults that have a difficult time fitting into daily routines on planet Earth. It is especially beneficial for star children, indigos, and walk-ins. It helps strengthen healers and teachers, and if you are assimilating recovered soul pieces or clearing Akashic issues, kunzite will comfort you and ease the transition period.

It is also a very protective stone that has the power to dispel negativity around you. Try it in your car to protect you from other drivers and keep you calm. Helpful in reducing stress related anxiety, Kunzite is excellent for panic attacks. It also helps dispel the effects of geopathic stress.

Physically, it is used for calming epilepsy, soothing joint pain and stimulates the immune system. This crystal is recommended for reducing depression, mood swings, stress, radiation. Good for the circulatory system and the lungs. A soothing stone that can help you adjust to the pressures of modern life.

Meditation to Yellow & White Kunzite

Close your eyes and relax. Take some nice, deep calming breaths and imagine that you are filled with a swirling pink and yellow light, easing through your cells and your body, suffusing your entire body, your entire being with peace and love, joy and happiness. Allow these loving, joyful feelings to radiate out from all your chakras. Your root chakra. Your sacral chakra. Your solar plexus. Your Heart. Your Throat. Your Third Eye. Your Crown. See the pink and yellow light filling you, filling the room, filling the world. See everyone you love filled with the same light. See everyone, everywhere you went today, filled with pink and yellow light. See the cities around you filled with pink and yellow light. See Washington DC, Montreal and Jerusalem filled with pink and yellow light. See the world glowing pink and yellow from afar.

Now imagine that you are connected to everyone in this room by a stream of flowing energy, flowing in and out of your third eyes like a shining white ribbon, flowing around the room in a circle. Feel the calming energy of Source entering you through the back of your head at the base of your skull, radiating through your body, and streaming out of you through the front of your forehead at your third eye. Feel the wonderful energy connecting each of you through your third eyes. Allow the love and connectedness to flow through your crown, your third eye, your heart and your soul. Feel the light and the love of Source, of the Holy Spirit, surround you. Know that you can feel this love and connection at any time, with anyone.

You are whole, and you are blessed. Now focus on your stone. What would you like to say to it? What would it like to say to you? Does it have any messages, or a name? Spend some time now communing with your piece of Kunzite, with your piece of heaven.

Now focus your light and your love on your own being. Bring all your light into yourself. Bring your silver cord back into yourself. Call in your pink light, your yellow light, your love and your joy. Wrap yourself up in your love and joy.

You are whole. You are one.

Return.

Hosting Your Own
Crystalline Club
or
Stone of the Month Group

It is very simple to host a monthly stone group. You don't have to be an expert, and you can easily learn along with your group.

The format my own group has always followed is to begin by discussing how the stone from the month before affected us, if we noticed any benefits or strange effects. Often, once everyone has shared, we see a common thread from the stones' influence!

Next, we pass around handouts describing what the stone is generally used for, where its from, what its made of. At the same time, I pass around a small bag filled with that month's stone – this way, everyone picks their stone by feel, not by how pretty or sparkly it is. Once everyone has a stone, I go over the handout.

Now for the fun part – we all meditate with our stones as a group. You can use the guided meditations given in this book, write your own or just sit quietly in silent meditation.

Finally, everyone gets to share what we experienced and any messages we might have received from our stones.

Remember, the stones are happy to be working with you. They have been waiting to co-create reality with you, to be held in your hand, to walk with you in your pocket.

Enjoy the magic, and get ready to watch your dreams unfold!

About the Author

Maya Cointreau is a certified Reiki master in the Usui tradition, herbalism and a shamanic lightworker with over 20 years of experience. She has been collecting rocks and seeking to know their inner secrets for four decades.

See more of her work at www.earthlodgebooks.com

More Earth Lodge Books:

Shades of Valhalla

Palm Reading for Everyone

Faerie Lost and Found

The Practical Reiki Symbol Primer

The Healing Properties of Flowers

The Comprehensive Vibrational
Healing Guide

The Mudra Book

Grounding and Clearing

The Girls Who Could Series

Energy Healing for Animals

Equine Herbs & Healing

Natural Animal Healing

www.ingramcontent.com/pod-product-compliance
Lightning Source LLC
Chambersburg PA
CBHW031946090426
42739CB00006B/103